The Slum Dweller

BY GERARD RILEY

"Give me the boy till 7…….
and I'll show you the man"

Recommended
Adult reading

ISBN 978095531742-2

Tootsie Rose Publishing
ENGLAND

Printed in Great Britain by
the MPG Books Group, Bodmin and King's Lynn

THIS BOOK IS DEDICATED TO THE MANY
THOUSANDS OF SLUM DWELLERS
BORN IN THE 1940's

Charlie Riley was born in County Antrim, Belfast, Northern Ireland in 1942.

Early in 1944, after his mother did a runner, he moved with his father and three brothers, the oldest of which was Jack, who was eight years old at the time, to Birmingham, England, the land of plenty. The only downside to this great adventure was that shortly before departing from Belfast, his father Frank had taken up with a little fat woman called Minnie.

She had four children of her own, much older than Charlie's family, the eldest of whom was a girl in her early twenties called Eva who the Riley boys renamed 'Eva the Evil' – along with two other sisters Marta and Rosie who did their limited best to help the younger half of their new family.

Last but not least was Minnie's son Sam who was in his early teens. To this day, the brothers believe he wasn't a full shilling.

What makes it even more interesting is the fact that half the Riley family was Catholic, and the other half Protestant!

CHAPTER 1

The Slum Dweller

Good old 1944 – the first time I remember being sick! It was on the ferry from Belfast to England and if I had known what awaited me I would have saved it in a paper bag for later consumption.

On reaching England, we settled in the Midlands, Birmingham to be precise, and Moseley in particular, where we ended up, living in three rooms of a large house on Trafalgar Road. The house itself consisted of a dozen rooms or more and at the time of us moving in, there were a couple of families already living there.

One of the things that has always stuck in my mind was the dilapidated bathroom on the first floor, with its rusted iron bath and the lath and plaster hanging from the ceiling – which always frightened the shit out of me, so needless to say I would only use it when I couldn't find anywhere else.

I would like to take a minute or two to introduce you to what I can only describe as my two half families.

There was my old man who was called Francis Riley. I bet he got some stick at school with a name like that, well I hope he did! Then there was myself, our Jack, our Jimmy, and last but not least our Sean.

The other half were called the Kelly's who we realized as time went by, were mainly a shower of Shit!

My stepmother's name was Minnie and I can only describe her as a fat, horrible, little woman who once my brothers and I got to know her a little, would always be referred to as 'The Fat Cow', but we were at all times very careful only to use our chosen name, when we were well away from the house, and her family!

Getting back to the rest of the Kelly's, the eldest daughter was called Eva who at that time would have been somewhere in the region of 18 to 20 years of age. She was 'one of them', you know the type – thinks she is better than anybody else, even to the point of trying to talk posh in a Belfast accent – but in truth was thicker than two short planks.

Then came Marta and Rosie, their ages around fourteen and fifteen, who were the only two of Minnie's kids who ever tried to make life better for me and my brothers.

Last, but not least, was Minnie's only son Sam, who was two or three years older than my eldest brother' and as it turned out as time went by, was as mean if not meaner than his mother.

As bad as they were, there was even more hassle to come our way on the religious side of things. They were Protestant and we were Catholic! What a bloody mixture. The devil himself could not have brewed a better one.

I don't remember much of what happened to me between two and four years of age, except I was always hungry, and kept wondering who the fuck I was. Incidentally from time to time I still do!

When I was four years of age, I started at the local Catholic school, where I seemed to stand out from most of the other kids, probably because I had holes in my trousers, and wore Wellington boots that gave me permanent black and red sore rings around my legs, but I suppose in retrospect I shouldn't complain as there were a lot of other kids as badly dressed as I was, and those of course were the ones I made friends with.

I had only been there for a short time when I became ill with a plague that was going around at the time, called impetigo. It was just my bloody luck to catch it.

The symptoms came in the form of scabs all over the body, which had to be painted with a blue lotion, and covered with bandages.

Just imagine for a moment if you can, your four year-old son, staggering down the road to school with scabby legs in Wellington boots, with holes in his trousers, and the rest of his body covered in dirty bandages. What a fucking sight for sore eyes!

The Money Lenders

The owners of the house where we lived were of Jewish stock, and lived across the road from us. From time to time Minnie would send me over with money to give to them, I found out later that they were repayments on £20 loans, for which she had to repay £22.

On most of these occasions, after giving them the money, the lady of the house would take me into her kitchen, and give me a large piece of home-baked cake' and just the taste of it was like being in heaven. In fact, I would go so far as to say from that day to this I have never tasted the likes.

It was to be many years later before I found out the reason for her kindness towards me, and that was only by accident.

It happened one time when Minnie once again sent me over with a payment. I might mention that on all previous occasions that I had taken money over to them, I would enter through a side door in the garden wall which brought me to the rear door of their house which, incidentally, was in an old fashioned conservatory. I would normally knock on the conservatory door and wait for them to open it, but on this occasion it was wide open, and although I couldn't see them, I could hear them.

Suddenly I was stopped in my tracks when I heard them arguing. After a moment or two I realized that they were discussing Minnie and my old man, with the old lady telling her husband to stop loaning money to her until she started to look after us and feed us properly, while adding that she was off a good mind to report both of them to the authorities for neglecting us.

After a minute or two, her husband quietened her down by saying if they stopped lending her money the kids would probably get even less to eat, and concerning the authorities they would be a total waste of time. After hearing what they had said, I quickly retraced my steps to the conservatory door and commenced to knock on it as hard as I could.

I have never forgotten that day, mainly for two reasons it was the first time I knew for sure that there were other people in the world who loathed my old man and Minnie, not just me and my brothers, and secondly because it was the biggest piece of cake I had received up until then.

Quite often after my eavesdropping incident while lying in bed with my three brothers, all in the same one, I would dream that the lady across the road had adopted us, and we wouldn't have to look at fat Minnie ever again. We should be so Bloody lucky!

My stepbrother Sam was twelve years older than me, and a real shit. He was big for his age, in both shit and body, and a bully to boot. What do you think of that for a fine description of an Irish gentleman?

His mother Fat Minnie pampered him, and he always had plenty to eat while my brothers and I had barely enough to keep us alive. On top of that he always wore nice clothes while we were dressed like tramps. However, I might add that, where Sam was concerned, he received his comeuppance in later years, in no uncertain way!

When I was six years of age, my best mate in school was called Patrick, but he was better known around the school by his nickname, 'The Stink' which didn't go down very well with him, needless to say. You will probably have guessed by now the reason behind his nickname – he was constantly farting, and on regular occasions would stink the classroom out. But what a Character! The teachers dreaded having him in their classroom, and would quite often make him stand out in the hallway until the end of the lesson. I found out later that the main reason for his regular stench was the fact that he lived on cabbage a large percentage of the time. In fact, the stench got so bad at one time that the headmaster sent his parents a note' asking them to cut down on his cabbage portions!

At that time in our Country's great history which would have been around 1948 – a lot of us suffered from malnutrition, bugs, bed and body scabs, lice, etc. but of course Patrick had to go one further, he was that kind of chap. If I remember correctly, it happened just before we broke up for the summer Holidays.

As usual, at break-time we would congregate with our mates, but this particular one sticks in my mind as it was some-what different from the norm. We were gathered around chatting away to one another when Patrick in his loud voice – which, by the way, he was also famous for! Invited us to form a circle around him so that he could show us his worms! First of all he showed us his forehead which had a few lumps and bumps on it, and one of the kids piped up that he had lumps a lot bigger than Patricks. This brought a smile to Patricks face 'You ain't got lumps like these, Mickey! Come on, take a look!' Patrick answered as he squeezed one, and a horrible looking worm slithered out of it.

'And I bet you can't do this either, Mickey' he added as he commenced to put it into his mouth and chew on it.
We could not believe what he had done with the worm, what a dirty git! Mind you, I suppose you really have to be starving to even contemplate eating a thing like that, but as uncouth as he was, in retrospect most us relied on him to make us laugh, and you can rest assured we really did need to in the 1940s!

It was about the same time as Patrick chewed his worm that we started to play with our willies to see who had the biggest! And I have no doubt you will know who the winner was. Yes, as always it was Patrick, who was far larger than any of us. When one of the kids asked him why he had a much bigger one than anyone else, he said it was because of all the cabbage he ate. That just about put the cap on it' and for the next two or three weeks most of the other Kids were on to their mothers to give them more cabbage! (Except of course yours truly)

A Real Education

I had just turned eight years of age when a couple of mates and myself started playing truant and we would wonder around Moseley stealing what we could from the local shops.

Our standard procedure would be for one of us to ask the shopkeeper for directions while the other two would fill their pockets with anything they could get their hands on.

Our favourite of course, was anything we could eat, as it was the only thing that had any value to us at that time in our lives.

At about the time I started thieving, another Irish family moved into the house. They were called Tom and Melia and had two young boys about two or three years old, and two daughters of a similar age to myself.

Tom, it seemed, worked alongside my old man and had done so for a few years. He was a funny little man in so much as he had a hump on his back, and walked a bit funny. On the other hand, Melia was taller than her husband and looked a bit on the blousy side, and liked a drink.

On reflection, I must admit that when I first met her, she looked like a movie star compared to Fat Minnie, and her daughters weren't bad either.

After a couple of weeks I had got to know their kids, and they started to invite me and my younger brother Jimmy up to their rooms to play. As time went by, I got to know Melia a lot better, so much so that she would send me to the off-license armed with an empty bottle for some draught beer, and I would sit in her room chatting to her as she supped it. Most of the time, my younger brother Jimmy would be with me, and she would tell us about her life, and the farm she was brought up on, with the happiest day of her life being the one' when she packed her bags and left, never to return.

Reading between the lines, she had obviously had a worse life than we were having, but it never seemed to get her down, in fact, we found her hilarious most of the time and added to that was the fact that she quite often found us a slice of bread and dripping.

Where her own kids were concerned they wanted for nothing - be it food, clothes or a mother's love, and I am glad to say that she lived to the grand old age of 92. That was one woman who did have a heart of gold! Anyway, that's enough of this soppy stuff, so let's get back to the normal way of things, and the 'good way of life' I and my brothers was living.

Our First Council House

When I was nine years old, Birmingham City Council gave us a three-bedroom house in St. Mary's Street in the area of Ladywood where my three brothers and I slept in the Attic in a large old bed, with a big bow in the middle.

As it happened it wasn't as bad as it sounds, as it had one redeeming feature. Once you were in the bed, you couldn't fall out! The only downside to this was that there was always the possibility of being crushed to death.

To stop this happening, my two eldest brothers would sleep in the dip in the centre and my younger brother and I would sleep at each side. (Ee lads! They were the good old days.) Mind you, with a bed like we had, who needed central heating? And I suppose even then we might have had a few problems if we had been a bit on the Gay side' there would certainly have been a few of sore bums in the family!

The New Neighbourhood

It didn't take us long to get to know most of our Neighbours, and what an interesting shower they were.

Next door to us there was a family of fifteen kids who, by their accents, had obviously emigrated from Wolverhampton. One of the things that will always stick in my mind was the fact that they drank their tea out of jam jars, that were always full to the brim.

It was because of this that everybody in the street looked down on them, and called them 'Dossers' or words to that effect. One of the main reasons for this attitude was because we, and they, thought we were Posher than them because we drank our tea out of proper little chipped and cracked cups' which by the way only held a quarter of the tea that a jam jar did. You wouldn't believe the mentality of the working class in those days! And God forbid' but if by some strange happening I was returned to that time' along with knowing what I know now' I would have mugged one of them for their Jam jar full of tea!

Another interesting thing about them was that their father kept chickens, loads of them, in his back yard with the majority of them being covered in scabs, and it didn't take fat Minnie long to decide that despite all the abuse she had given them, she would never the less like to try one!

After bribing me with an extra crust of bread to steal one, and wring its neck, she decided she would cook it for her and her family the following Sunday.

I might add at this juncture that from the moment fat Minnie came into our lives our staple diet was sliced bread (they only had thin sliced in those days) with the dreaded Echo Margarine, and on the odd occasion there would be Potatoes and cabbage. Even to this day whenever I see or smell cabbage I feel like pukin! Added to this delicious meal, as we began to get older the she would sometimes add a slice of Spam or Corned Beef. This went on until we left school and started to bring some money in. However, I am glad to say that she received the same from me, and my brothers, as she had given us! Since that fateful day when our old man, had been dragged between her fat flabby legs, and daft enough afterwards to take up with the fat cow….nothing!

The Oratory School (R.C)

The only Catholic school in the area was called the Oratory, and was much stricter than my previous one, but the schoolgirls more than made up for it - they were nicer looking, not that they took any notice of me, apart from of course making remarks concerning the state of my clothes.

By this time my mind had begun to awaken to new thoughts and feelings! And now and then my somewhat small penis would become hard and needless to say I would masturbate! At the same time that my erections were beginning in earnest, I still wore my short trousers with loads of patches on them along with my famous Wellington boots - trade mark and all - but even that thank God, didn't stop me fantasizing on seeing a good looking girl in the play ground, the things I would like to do to her…not that I had any real idea of what that was!

A crowd of us used to stand together on occasions watching the girls purposely jumping around so their little tits and bums would shake and jiggle, trying to turn us on, and invariably they would succeed, so it was off to the toilets for a 'J. Arthur. Rank' which was the local nickname at the time for masturbation, and discuss what we would like to do to them, given half the chance.

Any of you normal men out there who says he didn't have a 'J.Arthur' over a schoolgirl while he was at school is telling fibs or was unlucky! And missed the sexual awakening which to me and my mates was one of the best times in our mediocre lives.

The favourite class for most of the kids was French, not that any us ever learnt much, as we were too busy ogling the teacher' who incidentally, was a French woman!
She was about five foot two with lovely big tits and a beautifully shaped arse, and to our young eyes she looked beautiful, but on reflection, I do believe that she thoroughly enjoyed a load of young lads ogling her every movement. The girls didn't like it one bit – and it was easy for us to see why! They were obviously jealous of her big Tits.

The Arse Wacka!

The headmaster of the school was a right pig, for want of a better expression, and would have you in his office at your slightest misdemeanour, in order to enjoy his favourite pastime, whacking kids' bare arse's with his bamboo cane, while their trousers were around their ankles,.

In those days, the beginning of the 1950s, there were no such things as underpants as far as the working class was concerned, and I believe that if there had been, he would have had them off as well!

I had noticed on several occasions when dropping my trousers in front of him that he would wait for a few seconds or two before starting to whack my Arse. I did not realize at the time what he was doing or why, it was only years later when I had learnt a bit more about life that I realized that he was giving my rear end a good coat of looking at, and that it was quite possible that he was one of those weirdoes that we hadn't heard about at that particular time in our lives. I suppose, taking it all in all' that Headmaster and his cane must have seen and beaten more Kids Arseholes' than a thousand Paedophiles put together!

Most of the teachers in those days were upper middle class and one particular habit they had was that when the pupils entered their classroom, they would invariably direct the better dressed kids to the front and the scruffs, of which of course I was one, to the rear, and as far away from them as it was possible to be!

There was only ever one exception to the rule, and that was the English lessons which were run by an elderly lady teacher by the name of Mrs Pemm, who I realized in later years must have been a socialist, because she always put the scruffs at the front of her's.

CHAPTER TWO

Religion

Where religion was concerned the teachers and priests were, as I can only describe, similar to Nazis in forcing their doctrine down the pupil's throats, in every way, shape and form…which incidentally at times included violence!

Every Sunday, our old man would send us to Mass under threats of a good strapping if we didn't go. This, by the way, only applied to three of us, that being our Sean, our Jimmy and myself. Our eldest brother, Jack who was by that time older and big enough to tell the old man to fuck off and shove his religion up his arse!, was exempt.

But I am glad to say that even his threats didn't stop us from playing the wag on numerous occasions. Just think about it for a minute or two, and try to imagine kneeling with bare knees on a hard wooden platform for three quarters of an hour, listening to some old guy babbling away in a religious language that you understand very little of, and nine times out of ten you can bet your life that the same old bugger is still half pissed from the previous night.

The priests and the Catholic fraternity, on the whole, even to this day, drink large amounts of red wine, almost with every meal, and it would not surprise me if that included breakfast!

Monday Morning Assembly

Every Monday morning at assembly one of the priests would pick a handful of pupils and ask each of them which Mass they had attended the previous day, and more importantly what colour vestments had been worn by the priest at that particular one!

I will just take a minute to explain to you what normally happens in Catholic churches every Sunday. The first mass will begin somewhere near eight o'clock in the morning if not before. There will then follow, for at least four or five hours, numerous other Masses non-stop, every 30 to 45 minutes with the priest and the altar boys wearing different coloured clothing to each and every mass of that day.

While being questioned by the priest, and being unfortunate enough to get the colour wrong (whether you had been to church or not) you were sent directly to the Arse whacka's office for six of the best.

Oh boy! What a wonderful religion it is' when youngsters get the Shit knocked out of them for not going to Mass, or even going but not being able to remember the bloody colours.

A New Direction

Sometime around my 13th birthday, me and a couple of mates played the wag from school, and while looking for somewhere to rob, we came across a large combined vicarage and church, if I remember correctly it was called St John's. It didn't take us more than a minute or two to spot an open window at the rear of the property, but to be on the safe side, one of my mates knocked on the front door, on some pretence or other to find out if anyone was at home.

After knocking half a dozen times, and without receiving an answer, we decided to give it a go!

The only things we found worthwhile were in the kitchen, the most interesting of the two being the Gas Meter, which took only a moment or two to break open, but our luck was out, it had recently been emptied and there was only a few pence in it. After rummaging through the cupboards the only other things worth nicking were two packets of biscuits, which I suppose was better than a kick in the arse.

But unknown to us at that moment in time our luck was about to change! It happened on our way out, that one of my mates spotted a large built-in cupboard in an alcove, almost next to the window we had come through' and on a closer inspection, he found a red biscuit tin on the top shelf, which he managed to get hold of by climbing on one of the chairs' and surprise, surprise, it was half full of money which had obviously come from the Sunday collection's.

It consisted of pennies, half pennies, sixpences, etc. You probably won't believe me when I say' that to us, it was like winning the football pools.

Once we were away from the crime scene, and after scoffing our biscuits, we decided unanimously to leave home, there and then, for pastures new!

Leaving Home

That same evening we ended up in Balsall Heath, which was the main area at that time where the immigrants, mostly Pakistanis had settled.

After wandering around for an hour or two, we found an empty, bombed out house, which was just one of many that had never been rebuilt after the war, and settled down for the night, content in the knowledge that we had a load of money in our pockets, and a bright future in front of us.

It must have been around five or six in the morning when we awoke shivering with the cold, and viewed our new lodgings. God! What a bloody dump we had ended up in! There were piles of rubbish everywhere, rats running all over the place, and large holes in the roof. It was quite obvious from the piles of human shit all over the place that it had been used by other squatters before us. What a fucking way to start our new lives!

By the end of the second day, we were running out of money and knew that we would have to start thieving the following day in order to survive, and keep our freedom.

By evening we had found a much better squat than our previous one, and settled down for the night, content in the knowledge that we were now seasoned burglars, and would have no problem surviving as long as we stuck together.

The Coppers

It was three o'clock in the morning when we were awoken by two six foot coppers, but fair play to them, as soon as we reached the police station they gave us a nice cup of hot tea.

However, they then tried to get us to confess to other burglaries which they knew we hadn't committed, I suppose where the police trade is concerned, it was worse in that era as compared to nowadays, but nevertheless the system was the same concerning their promotional procedures, as in the more crimes they solved, the quicker their promotion, and it didn't particularly bother them whether they had the right person or not.

After being grilled for two or three hours by the C.I.D. and refusing to admit to other crimes that we hadn't committed, even though they had given us a few slaps around the head trying to make us change our mind, they ended up charging us with breaking and entering, and the judge sent all three of us to a remand home for three weeks, with my old man having to pay something towards my upkeep.

As no doubt you can imagine from the description of my old man previously given to you, on hearing this from the judge he went into a rage, and threatened to kill me when I came out, but Lady Luck was smiling on me that day, for a change I might add.

The judge had overheard him say this to me and severely reprimanded him, telling him, in no uncertain way that under no circumstances was he to use violence towards me in any shape or form, as I was already being punished by the courts by being sent to a remand home.

My old man, by the way, wasn't angry with me being sent to the remand home. Oh no, it was because he would have to part with some of his beer money for the next three weeks, and just knowing that made my day.

After being told off by the judge it was very rare in the future for him to lift his hand or belt to me. Don't get me wrong, there were many times when it took all of his willpower to stop himself from doing so!

The Remand Home

The home was situated in an area called Moseley Heath, which was very near to the place where we had previously slept rough. It was a very large house in its own grounds, housing between 25 and 30 juveniles and was run by a Catholic Brotherhood called the de la Salle.

On our arrival, my mates and I weren't too worried after all because of the way we had lived up until then. Nothing frightened us, or so we thought!

What a surprise we had on entering the home! First off, we had to take a shower (My first one ever) after which we were given smart clean clothes – trousers with no arse hanging out' then we were taken to the Matron to see if there was anything wrong with us. From there, we were taken to our dormitory, where there were six beds with beautiful clean sheets. Until that time in my life I had never slept in a bed with sheets on.

We were then instructed on how to make our beds, in a uniform fashion.

When tea time arrived we couldn't believe the amount of food we received. Compared to what the three of us were used to, it was like a feast, and on top of that we received a large cup of cocoa before going to bed.

The next morning, after a good night's sleep, we were awoken at 6am and immediately made our beds in the fashion we had been shown the previous day, had a good wash and cleaned our teeth, that being the first time I had ever done so in my life.

All of this was done at the double, and anyone not moving quickly enough received a whack on the arse from a cane to help them on their way. The way they used the cane reminded me of the arse whacker at the oratory school. Who knows? Perhaps they were related in some way. We then assembled for breakfast, which consisted of porridge followed by scrambled egg on toast, or something similar.

At the time I just could not believe this was happening to me, and in fact it did cross my mind that perhaps I could ask the judge to double my sentence. Can you just imagine my old man's face, having to fork out some more of his beer money for an extra three weeks of this?

After breakfast, we assembled in the yard, where everyone was dispersed to their particular sections such as gardening. By the way they not only grew all their own fruit and vegetables, but on top of that grew extra to sell directly to the public. As well as the gardening section, they had a building section consisting of repairs, painting and decorating, plus most of the other trades that was necessary for the maintenance needed to keep the home in good repair.

With my two mates being big lads, they were automatically placed in the building section, and yours truly, being on the small side, on the gardening section. So during the day, we saw very little of one another.

At dinner time we stopped for thirty minutes for a sandwich and a cup of tea and when the half-hour was up, we were marched back to work, at the double, and by tea-time most of us were completely knackered.

The first stop was the showers, followed by our evening meal and on finishing that we were dispersed to a large compound with outbuildings where we could play table tennis and dominoes, or just stand around talking to one another. By the way there was no seating of any kind.

The Cock!

As in every school there is always what we called at the time 'The Cock of the school' (which bore no relation to the penis whatsoever). Of course there are always contenders for this position, even more so with the large turnover of lads coming in and going out, with sentences ranging from three to six weeks, which invariably caused many more clashes of personality than it would in a normal school life, (where the majority are there for much longer) thus allowing the tensions to be more settled, especially where the violence is concerned.

The maximum age for lads in those days was fifteen and you had better believe me, when I tell you that some real hard cases came through those gates, and there is no doubt in my mind that a small percentage in later years would become gangsters

The fights for power always took place in the toilets where there was plenty of room for the spectators, who invariably would bet on the outcome with anything they had such as chocolate or polo mints.

One of these fights took place shortly after our arrival. The existing cock, nicknamed 'The Rat', had been challenged by a newcomer for the Crown! This newcomer was built like a brick shithouse' while on the other hand, the Rat was much smaller, with a slim, muscular body and a pair of hands like hammers, but needless to say because of the newcomer's size most of the bets were on him.

The Financial Setup

Before I continue any further I must explain something to you concerning the financial set-up in this kind of institution, it being similar to those used in most other Government institutions' of the day.

Each Sunday morning, the inmates would receive pocket money for his week's work, which was, in fact, a credit in the school sweet shop, but before receiving it, there would be reductions for any misdemeanours committed during that week.

The shop opened for one hour each Sunday morning. On top of this, all inmates were allowed visitors for one hour every Sunday afternoon, that being the only time when they were allowed to receive food parcels from their families, so this of course, brought more revenue into the betting, whether it be table tennis, dominoes, fighting or anything else for that matter, that the lads might find of interest. Needless to say there were never any visitors for yours truly, or my mates for that matter.

Getting back to the fight; all fights took place after our evening meal in our recreation time, with a couple of lads having to keep watch for the house master.

When my mates and I arrived at the toilets, the show was ready to hit the road, but alas it didn't last very long. The Rat proceeded to smash one of his big fists into the big fellow's jaw, followed by a kick in the cobblers and a boot either side of his head as he hit the deck! Job finished in thirty seconds! And we all went back to the dominoes and table tennis.

The De La Salle Brotherhood

Concerning the De La Salle brothers who ran the school, you would have a very hard time finding a bigger shower of creeps anywhere on God's earth.

There were ten of them, and at all times they travelled in pairs, and according to the grapevine, some of the younger lads went missing from their dormitories for a few hours each night, but when questioned by the other lads they would pretend that they didn't know what they were talking about. Mind you, I suppose I should be grateful, for once in my life, that I was a skinny little bastard. And I am sure that because of that' they would have had a hell of a job getting a lob on while looking at me, so perhaps that was my saviour in disguise.

If you had to speak to one of the brothers for any reason, you addressed him as 'Bruv' as in 'Yes Bruv, no Bruv, three bags full Bruv'.

The housemaster went by the name of Ignatious. He was in the region of five foot eight inches in height, stockily built, and was a very mean and nasty person. God help anyone who crossed him and I think that included God himself!

One evening, after tea, a few of us were talking to him in the recreation area, when one of the lads said something a little sarcastic. The next instant he was on the ground with his face covered in blood, and his front teeth hanging out. Ignatious was kicking him all over his body, he was like a maniac, screaming and swearing, and had it not been for one of the other brothers pulling him off, the lad would have been dead! Needless to say he ended up in the sick bay for a good many days! So much for Gods Disciples! Needless to say, most of us steered clear of him after that.

Do you ever find when you are waiting for a certain day to come, it never seems to! Especially when you have only a few days left on your sentence? But thank God it invariably does, and you're back on the outside. Even when you are leaving the best food you have ever had in your life' its not a patch on your freedom! And I knew when I walked out of the gate that I would never return!

My Home Coming

When I arrived home to the family's chateau, neither the old man or my stepmother, Fat Minnie said 'hello' to me, or even 'how are you son? Nice to have you home! It was as though I wasn't there, or had never gone away – take your pick. How nice it is to have loving parents! The only time the old man spoke to me after that was when I caused him more hassle, and I invariably did.

It was only a short time after I had come out of the remand home that my older brother Sean got in trouble with the police, and was sent to what they called, in those days, an approved school, for twelve months (they call them Detention Centre's nowadays). I was a bit sick about it, as I could always rely on him to get me out of trouble where arguments and fighting was concerned.

By this time, my younger brother Jimmy had made plenty of friends of his own age. In fact, he had turned out to be quite a good looking young lad, and didn't really look like a Riley. It did cross my mind over the next couple of years, that before our mother did a runner, that she might have had what some people call nowadays a 'love child' while she was still living with our old man. By the way it used to be called a bastard in those days, but anyway, what the fuck does it matter where each of us has come from?

After all, we had all served our time in hell, or something near to that, under the ministrations of Fat Minnie and our old man.

CHAPTER THREE

The Sexual Awakening

After that bit of information I will get back to when I was fourteen, and what was going on then.

Our Sean, who had just arrived home from the approved school, and I started to knock about with a lad that lived further down our street called Mickey.

Mickey was certainly a one-off in as much as he was as hard as nails, and without an ounce of fear in him. He was a real macho looking guy, and could pull the girls by the dozen. To top that off, he had the right place to take them.

At the time of this happening he was eighteen years of age, and lived with his family over a storage depot warehouse, where he was employed as a store man for the same canned food company that owned both the accommodation he and his family lived in, and the depot underneath.

His job consisted of loading, and unloading, mainly small vans for dispersal of their tinned goods to their outlets over the north of England, but the most interesting part was that he ran the small warehouse on his own' from opening in the morning until closing in the evening.

On top of that, and the fact that he was living in the flat above the warehouse, he was expected to provide a bit of security for the well-being of the warehouse and its contents' after which, he could do what he wanted, within reason.

As I got to know Mickey better, I asked him one day while our Sean wasn't around, if I could sometimes hide in his warehouse and spy on him while he was fucking his lady friends. On hearing this from a 'scrawny young lad' he burst out laughing and called me a 'cheeky little Bastard' but never the less, said he would think about it!

During the school holidays I would help him to load the vans, clean up the warehouse, and give him a hand with his stock taking. For this help he would give me a shilling, along with plenty of sandwiches. It was certainly one of the better phases in my life.

Whether I was at school or not, I would always clean up the warehouse on a Saturday morning, come rain or shine.

While locking up one Saturday dinnertime, about three weeks after I had asked' if I could spy on him, he told me to be at the warehouse at seven o'clock that same evening, as he was meeting a married woman whose husband was in the army, and hadn't been home for four or five weeks, and he knew for sure that she wanted him to shag her.

I think I must have had a hard-on most of the afternoon thinking about seeing the real thing for the first time in my life.

By the way, there had been the odd time when, on making my way up and down from the attic, that I had sometimes caught a glimpse of the old man grunting and groaning while lying on top of Fat Minnie with his long johns down around his ankles, "when he had forgotten to close his bedroom door" On occasions like that, I felt like puking' In fact it was enough to put a young lad off sex for the rest of his life!

The Real Thing

I was there at seven on the dot! And to say I was feeling nervous and excited, is an understatement, but after ten minutes of hanging about there was still no sign of Mickey, and I was beginning to think that he had set this up to take the piss out of me' or was it because the woman hadn't turned up for their date? As these terrible thoughts were going through my mind, he walked around the corner and when he saw me, he burst out laughing.

I bet you thought I wasn't coming you little sod! While adding in a threatening voice that if I should ever open my mouth to any of my mates, he would rip my fucking head off!

That out of the way, and still with a smile on his face, he told me, 'that he didn't want half of the kids in the area hanging around the depot for their first sex lessons!'

My cock was already at half mast as we entered the warehouse, and after sorting me out a good spot where I would be able to see everything that went on, he burst out laughing on seeing my now rock hard cock making a tent in the front of my trousers.

As he was closing the door behind him he turned to me, still with a smile on his face and said, Charlie, while you're

having a wank, don't you dare make a sound! And by the look of your dick sticking out of your trousers, I would suggest, that while I am gone for a few minutes to pick her up, that you have yourself a quick 'J. Arthur ' otherwise you will be coming in your trousers before you see her!
The minute he was out of the door, I took his advice and did just that!

A Lesson On How To Do It

The lady in question wasn't as good looking as some of the girls I had seen him with, or as young, but never the less she was attractive, and she certainly wasn't fat like my stepmother. It didn't take Mickey long to get her clothes off. I think one of the things I liked about the scene, was her lovely pair of tits as they appeared. They were more exciting to me than anything I had ever been able to conjure up in my mind in the past, (while having a J. Arthur)

Even today, I can still see him taking her black suspender belt and nylons off, followed by her knickers, and exposing to my virgin eyes for the first time in my life, a woman's pubic hair. I remember thinking, 'How the Fuck will he be able to find her fanny underneath all that hair? Although I said in the beginning about her looks being on the average side, her naked body more than made up for that. It was gorgeous and the rock-hard cock in my hand was going ten to the dozen.

While stripping his young lady of her clothing, bit by bit, he had managed to do likewise to himself, and all I remember about his cock was that it was far larger than mine. I think mine must have become stunted through to much good living.

Suddenly out of the blue she knelt down on the sheet covered mattress, and took his cock into her mouth, and started sucking it. I couldn't believe what I was seeing.

Even in conversations with my mates, none of them had ever referred to women doing this to a man. I had thought in my ignorance that it was only those who we referred to as queers who did that sort of thing.

After a minute or two of sucking him, Mickey pulled her down to the mattress. By this time I was totally mesmerized by what was going on. I was now going to see what I would have to do, hopefully in the very near future, in order to get my cock into a girl's 'thingy' and by the look of all that hair, I thought Mickey was going to have a hard job on his hands, but I was very much mistaken as his cock suddenly, and completely, disappeared into her body, followed by squeals and moans coming from her mouth as his cock started going in and out of her faster and faster, with her squeals and moans getting louder and louder, and when she suddenly tried to buck him off, accompanied by a little scream, I knew without being told that she had reached her climax.

By the time I got home that night, apart from being totally knackered from all the 'J. Arthurs' I'd had while watching the show, unbeknown to me at that moment in time, a new window in my life had opened, and from that day forward my whole outlook on life had changed completely. Over the three or four months following my lesson on sex in the warehouse I was a different person, it was as though I had grown up overnight.

One of the first things that I noticed was the new confidence that had suddenly appeared in my mind and actions, and the loss of a great many inhibitions.

Recreation

On looking back to that era, the only recreational facilities for youngsters were the local Parks, and there wasn't many of them, those that did exist had nothing more than a few swings and roundabouts, and possibly a see-saw or two.

By the time you were nine or ten year-old even those had ceased to be a facility' which left them "the Parks" only being useful for a game of football, or at best a meeting place for hooligans.

Most of the working classes couldn't afford a television on the wages they earned, even though they were only black and white at the time, and I would go so far as to say that if Minnie had managed to buy one she would not have allowed me or my brothers to watch it. So, in retrospect, between the ages of 10 and 15 the only pastime activities open to kids were the swimming baths, if you could afford it, a game of football in the street or park, and If you were lucky, and I mean bloody lucky! you could listen to a football match on an old wireless, provided you were able to tune it in to the correct frequency for more than the normal five minutes at a time.

The only other thing I can think of, apart from doing a bit of nicking now and then, was to chase the girls. Then my friends, one of the best days of my life arrived, and I left school.

The Real World

It wasn't me, but my old man, who decided that I was to become an electrician. In those days you had to do a six month trial period before they would sign you on for a five-year apprenticeship. My starting wage was one pound nineteen shillings a week.

At the time there was very little I could do about it, knowing full well that until I was sixteen I couldn't tell him and Minnie to fuck off' once and for all!

At the time I started work, my mates were mostly working in factories earning anywhere between four and five pounds a week, so I have no doubt you can imagine how sick I was with my measly 39 shilling, with a large part of that having to go to sweet Minnie for my keep.

It was just after starting work in the electrical trade that the council offered Minnie and my old man a four-bedroom council house on a new overspill estate in the Castle Bromwich area of Birmingham, which in those days was a nice place to live, and until then had only housed what the working class referred to as 'posh' people.

There is no doubt in my mind that a few years later those posh Buggers in Castle Bromwich would rue the day that they had allowed, without a fight, the council to build those estates, Kingshurst and Chelmsley Wood.

But I must admit that on seeing the house for the first time, with its front and rear gardens, and a nice sized bathroom, I was very impressed by it all.

The house itself was slightly elevated which allowed Minnie to watch the bus stop to see when my old man got off the bus on his way home from work, knowing that most nights he would call into the Kingshurst pub for a beer or two before coming home for his evening meal.

On moving to Kingshurst, she splashed out on two new double beds for me and my three brothers, but alas not a bed sheet in sight, not that we really noticed at the time-I suppose that is what the old saying means, 'You rarely miss what you have never had'!

It didn't take me, Sean and Jimmy long to make friends. Most of the kids in their early teens had moved on to the new estate from every slum area that circled Birmingham town centre - Ladywood, Edgbaston, Nechells, Aston, Small Heath etc. - so basically most of them had come from a similar environment and found it easy to relate to each other.

After three or four weeks living in our new house, I began to get homesick for Ladywood and some of the friends I had left behind, even with knowing that most of them would have been moved by the council to one of the other estates that was still being built on the outskirts of Birmingham.

One example of this was the estate where my old friend Mickey and his family had been moved to, which was called Weoley Castle, and was the opposite outskirt of Birmingham to where I now lived, and would take in excess of an hour and a half by bus to reach, and as unlike the present there were no house phones in those days (not for the working class) to help keep you in touch with one another's movements.

Pissed Off

After using the bus backwards and forwards to the town centre for a few weeks and on top of that having to walk a mile across town to where I was working, which was the new multi-storey offices situated on Broad Street opposite the Granville pub, I was well and truly pissed off!

It was less than ten minutes walk from where I worked' to the part of Ladywood where I had previously lived. My main job on the site didn't help, as I was basically the tea and sandwich boy, and was learning sweet fuck all about the trade I was supposedly working in!

One evening when I was really pissed off, I told my old man I was going to jack my job in at the end of the week. As you can imagine he went 'Radio Rental' and told me in no uncertain terms that if I jacked it in, he would throw me out on my arse.

I decided to give the old man an hour to settle his brain down, and went for a walk to clear my head. It was only when I was walking that I realized that during our argument, while my old man was ranting and raving, that he had mentioned that he would throw me out if I didn't toe the line and I suddenly decided this was as good a time as any to get gone!

I returned to the house, went straight to my bedroom and packed everything I owned. In retrospect I don't know why I bothered, there was barely enough to fill a carrier bag. I then decided before I disappeared that I would let the old man know what I had always thought of him, so without any hesitation I walked into the living room where he and fat Minnie were sitting in front of their new black and white television.

The old man was just putting a glass of beer to his mouth, it was what they called in those days 'family ale' of which he drank two or three large bottles every evening after his meal' and without further ado I commenced to tell him what I thought of him, 'bastard' no doubt being just one of the words I used, along with 'drop dead you old twat' and finished off by telling him to fuck off!

I was out of the front door before what I had said to him having had time to sink in. Halfway to the bus stop I looked back and could see him shaking his fist while calling me all the names under the sun. It was to be a good many years before we would meet again.

Independence

I knew I would have a problem with the police concerning my age, as leaving home before sixteen years of age was against the law, but at that particular moment in time, I had much more important things to worry about, Money and lodgings being my number one concern!

It had been early in the week when I had left home, I think it was a Tuesday, but I certainly do remember my financial position at that particular time. I had five "Bob" to my name, and I would have to wait until Friday to pick up my week's wage of 39 shillings.

I had no option but to doss in one of the many derelict houses the first night. Early the next morning, after a wash and brush up in one of the the new local council-run underground toilets called 'Wash Ups' (combined facilities), I started to look at one or two of the boarding houses advertising full board, of which in those days, there were plenty knocking about, mostly used by Irish labourers working on the roads and building sites.

After visiting half a dozen or more, I found that most of them charged in the region of two pounds a week, payment in advance, which put me out of the running straight away, and the only option left open to me was to spend the next couple of nights dossing in the same place I had used the night before.

It was my intention within the next couple of days to find myself a better paying job to start the following week, which in those days was very easy to do.

In the early 50's, Birmingham was the largest industrial city in the world, so much so that you could walk out of one job and into another in one hour guaranteed! I know it's true, because I actually did so on a couple of occasions, a little later on.

After my couple of nights kipping rough, Friday came and even though I was starving I felt like King Kong, as I walked into the office to pick up my wages.

On seeing me the wages Clerk looked some what surprised, the first words out of his mouth being, 'What the fuck are you doing here? Your old girl came in half an hour ago and demanded your wages. I told her to bugger off Charlie, which she didn't take very kindly to! In fact, she said she wouldn't leave the premises until she had spoken to the boss, and if she had any problems with him she would call the fucking police.

With a helpless look on his face he said to me 'I am sorry mate, but there was nothing anyone could do under the circumstances, In fact, I threw the fucking packet at her, and told the fat cow to piss off out of my sight before I clobbered her. We didn't have a leg to stand on Mate, especially with you being under sixteen, as you know yourself Charlie, your parents have all your rights!'

No doubt you can imagine what I felt like at that moment in time, just turned fifteen, run away from home, no money, no digs, and not even enough money for a sandwich.

It felt like a bad dream, but in reality was more like a fucking nightmare which I half expected to wake up from any minute, but there was more to come. Minnie had mentioned to the Clerk that the police were out looking for me to take me back home. On hearing this, I forgot my other problems for a second or two as I sprinted out of the office, and didn't stop until I was half a mile away!

Our Kid

After wandering around the streets for an hour, feeling like one of the walking dead, I decided to make my way to the gasworks where our Sean worked.

My brother's main job was shovelling coke with a machine to feed the furnaces. The Company he worked for was based in Saltley Gas Works, about three miles outside the city centre.

Our kid loved his job, the pay was good, and his boss thought a lot about him. When I had finished telling him what had happened he said he would choke the old cow when he got home, and apparently, believe it or not, he was just about to do so when Minnie's son Sam walked in.

Sam was at least six years older than our Sean and had always fancied himself as a hard man, even more so after spending the past three years in the army where he had spent all of his spare time bodybuilding, and was now twice his original size.

He grabbed hold of our kid as though he was the famous bodybuilder Charles Atlas, and our kid commenced to knock ten kinds of shit out of him, leaving him unconscious on the front room lino with Fat Minnie screaming her head off.

At last the bully and his mother had reaped their just rewards; perhaps after all there is someone up there! And to finish it off, he managed to get thirty shillings of my wages off Minnie, and my old man never said boo!

While our kid had been sorting Minnie out, I stayed in his works canteen overnight. I say 'canteen' but really it was an old ramshackle tin hut, with loads of coats and wellies lying around, but the comforting part of it all was the little coke burner in the middle of the floor with its steel tube chimney disappearing through the roof overhead, and it turned out to be the best night's sleep I had had' in nearly a week.

The next day when our kid arrived at work, and gave me the thirty shillings. I was over the moon, but he had even more good news for me.

After decking Sam Kelly, he got on his motor bike, and set off to see his new girlfriend who lived in the part of Ladywood that wasn't being pulled down.

I think It was the first time that he had picked her up at her house, and while doing so, she informed him that their next door neighbour knew him and his family, and had told her the next time she met our kid to let her know' as she would like to have a chat with him to see how we had all gotten on, and also informed his girl that he could find her any evening across the road in the Bishopsgate public house. It turned out that it was no other than my old friend from the past, Melia the lady I used to fetch the beer for when we lived in Moseley.

Needless to say my brother ended up buying Melia and her husband Tom a couple of beers, and gave them an update on how we had gone on since we had seen them last. When he got around to my immediate problem concerning having to find digs in a hurry, and not having sufficient cash at that moment to do so, she told him to send me down right away to see her, and she would put me up on the Bed settee for a few days until I could sort myself out.

CHAPTER FOUR

When I arrived at Melia's, it felt to me like I was coming home! Don't you think it's a pity that these good feelings that we seldom get' never last? Well such is life!

It was great to see her again, and she took me over to the snug in the Bishopsgate Arms, where we had a couple of halves of beer, and a good chat. She loved to talk, and even more so where Minnie was concerned. She had despised her from the first day she had set eyes on her, and seen for herself the way she treated me and my brothers. I did notice that she never said a bad word about my old man, and referred to him in our conversation with what seemed to me to be fondness, which after a while gave me the feeling that there might have been something going on between them, I found out much later that there in fact, had been.

In later years when my old man and I became friends for the first time in our lives, I used to give him a right slagging for being a naughty boy, and throwing his dick around behind Minnie's back, but perhaps I should save that particular story until another time.

Getting back to Melia, she told me I was welcome to stay until I could afford to find a bed-sit of my own, but I would have to make do on the settee. Over all, I found sleeping on the settee more than all right.

The only downside to it was the fact that I could not go to bed until everyone else had, but nevertheless we have to be grateful for small mercies, and in my case I certainly was.

I think I should now give you an insight into Melia's kids, the eldest was Dora who was sixteen at the time, and courting a cockney lad' whom she later married when he put her in the Family way, poor bastard, and I don't mean her, but I must admit I fancied giving her one myself' on a few occasions. By the way, in those days the lads referred to it as 'lending them one'.

I must admit that on the odd occasion while living there I had the odd 'J. Arthur Rank' while thinking about what I would like to do to her. Dora was one of those girls who thought a lot of herself and let everybody in her circles know it – like bending over in front of you while you were sat on the settee, showing you the cheeks of her lovely little arse. I used to get a lob on just looking at her in that position, and I believe that is why she did it. The name we used for girls who acted like that' was a 'prickteaser'. We really did have! some charming ways of expressing ourselves!

Another pastime of hers was squeezing past me in the tiny kitchen or, as we called them in those days, sculleries. Apart from holding a small cast-iron gas cooker and a Belfast sink, there was only enough standing space left to accommodate two or three people at a push, and I believe she enjoyed rubbing her "tits" against me in passing.

Anyway I think that's enough vulgarity for the moment. Let's move on to Melia's two sons who were as different as chalk and cheese. Jonas was the eldest of the two, he would have been around eleven years of age when I first moved in, and was a real headcase. He was the type of boy who was always laughing, and causing some kind of hassle or other, unlike Donald his younger brother who was the last kind of boy you would ever adopt, even if he was the last one on the face of the earth! But alas his mother doted on him and would literally give him her last penny and when he had spent that, he would scream and throw tantrums for some more that he knew didn't even exist.

Melia's other daughter was called Nancy. Now this girl was a real beauty, about five foot two in height and she had the lot – lovely legs, lovely face, and a nice slim body. Needless to say, all the local lads were after getting into her knickers, but from what I heard a few years later she took up with a local man – about 35 years old, less than five foot tall, ugly! And on top of that was a Jamaican, and they had three kids in quick succession.

I do believe from knowing him quite well myself, that he had a dick like a donkey. It was just a pity that he looked like one. Sorry, mate! Anyone who says he understands women is talking out of his fucking arse! No disrespect to Jamaicans intended, but what a way for a beautiful young girl to end up, when she could have had any decent young lad in the surrounding areas.

It was to be ten years later when our Sean and I were talking over a beer about the good old days, most of which only started when we left Minnie behind. That he happened to mention that Nancy had left her Jamaican husband, it having happened shortly after she had met a sugar daddy who bought her a lovely apartment in one of the better parts of Birmingham, and to me that was the best news I could possibly have had concerning that young lady.

Now we come to the last, but not least, of the family Tom, the very hardworking husband and father of four kids.

As I have already mentioned at the beginning of the Book, he stood at five foot two with a large hump on his right shoulder. He had worked at the same company for donkey's years, and was very proud to be recognized as the fastest steelwork polisher in the factory. In being so, he had always earned the best money' as it happened it was just as well with the family he had, and his wife who liked a drink.

In thc week or so I was there, I got to know him fairly well. In fact after talking to him for a while he referred to the time that my old man had worked with him, while adding that he had not been the greatest of workers, but nonetheless he did class him as a mate. I think he might have changed his mind somewhat if he had found out that our old man Francis had been lending his wife one in earlier times.

By the way' my old man never gave much away, if you know what I mean. I think in those days, I would go so far as to say that he would charge you for giving you a dose of the clap! He was a real gent! In the short time I was there, I made one or two mates of my own age and started to settle down, and look around for a bed-sit in the same area.

I started my search by looking at adverts in the various shop windows for rooms to let, and found one.

It was a large Property on Wheeleys Road, and the Bedsit in question was situated on the ground floor at the rear of a large House.

When I knocked on the door I didn't know what to expect, all kinds of things were going through my mind, was he a Poofter?, a Weirdo?.. So you can imagine the look on my face when an old schoolmate from the past opened the door. In fact, he had been one of my best mates at school, I suppose him having a horrible stepmother similar to Minnie, if that's possible, helped to nurture our friendship at the time.

After a cup of tea and a chat it turned out that a couple of weeks after leaving school he had a fall out with his stepmother who was always the boss in the house. She was a lot younger than his father, and she had persuaded him "the father" to throw Jimmy out, which at the time suited him down to the ground, especially with him being under the age of sixteen.

The reason he was looking for someone to share the bed-sit was the fact that he was working on a five-year Apprenticeship as a tool maker and even though he was doing over time he was always struggling to pay the rent.

The Bedsit

The bed-sit was quite large as bed-sits go, it had a large bow window looking out over an over grown garden' a very large room with two single beds, a three-piece suite, a table and four chairs, and a fair sized Scullery which you had to step down to enter' the only thing that was of putting was its concrete floor, which no doubt would be bloody cold in winter time. Also in the scullery was an old gas cooker, and a very large shallow Belfast sink.

I will always remember that sink, probably because from that day to this I have never come across another like it, and probably more so for the fact that it was built in at the right height for pissing in.

You must bear in mind at that time in our lives both me and Jimmy were only around five foot tall, and the only toilet was at the top of the house, which was a long way from the ground floor, so in essence it was a bonus.

In that Era' it being the middle to late 50s there were very few houses with bathrooms, and even more so where digs were concerned, so it was off to the public baths at the end of the week when you had finished work, and you could even get something to eat in their cafeteria afterwards.

A couple of days before seeing the flat I had once again started a new job on a building site that paid good money, so I agreed to pay half of the outgoings and moved in to my own pad.

Although we had been good friends at school' and probably because our outlook on life was somewhat different' from day one we didn't see a lot of one another, but never the less every now and then we would have a couple of beers together.

It was shortly after moving in with Jimmy that the police found me, but once they knew I was working and had somewhere half-decent to live, plus the picture I painted for them of fat Minnie they let me stay. I think it helped them knowing that in a further six months I would be sixteen, and have my own rights.

The minute they had gone, Jimmy and I went out to the nearest pub and got pissed on three pints apiece. At eleven pence a pint, those certainly were the days, if only beer wise!

Wheeleys Road, where I now lived, was well-known as bed-sit land, and I believe that if you could reintroduce the same area, to nowadays as it was then, people would call it trendy and colourful, but what made it even better for me, it was only ten minutes walk from Melia's house, the area that my new mates lived.

A short time after moving in a woman's dead body was found nearby. And according to the papers she had been raped and strangled. The police were everywhere, including our bed-sit, but surprise surprise they didn't take us away, even though they informed us that the neighbours had told them that we had been seen by some of them bringing girls into the house.

The Breaking In!

One night, just after my sixteenth birthday, I stopped off on my way home from work with a couple of workmates at one of the pubs I had used in the past. After a couple of beers, my mates left and I got talking to one of our Seans mates, Pat was his name and he and his older brother worked for themselves in the demolition business.

As the night wore on' we or rather I, got drunker and drunker, and during our conversation I must have mentioned to Pat that a few days earlier had been my sixteenth birthday. On leaving the pub at closing time we decided to have a cup of coffee at an Expresso coffee bar that I used on a regular basis.

Pat was from Southern Ireland; by the way our Sean always knocked about with the Irish, even to this day they are his favourite people.

Pat was in his mid to late twenties with a mop of wavy black hair, and was married to a lovely looking woman, the odd times that you would see them out together would be on a Saturday night, and unless someone told you, you would never believe, looking at her, that she had borne him six kids.

During our conversation in the coffee bar, the topic of sex came up after I had made a remark or two about how I would love to give a certain young lady one! The young lady in question was sitting a few tables away from us, with two or three of her girlfriends. I had noticed that since we had entered the place she had been eying Pat up and trying to catch his eye, in between of which she would whisper to her mates' the obvious effect from her doing so had them giggling. When I mentioned this to Pat, he burst out laughing, saying he had more than he needed at home' where dipping his wick was concerned! Then out of the blue, he asked me point-blank if I had had my leg-over yet. If he had asked me the same question when I was sober I would have told him to piss off! But before I could answer, he seemed to know what I would say, no doubt by my now red face.

His next words again took me by surprise, 'Come on Charlie Riley, drink up I've decided to give you a treat for your birthday, and I am not telling you where we are going until we get there!'

By this time we had downed a couple of coffees and I was beginning to feel a bit more sober.

On leaving the coffee bar, Pat managed to flag a passing taxi on its way back to the town centre' and as we got into it he whispered into the driver's ear so I wouldn't know where he was taking me. We ended up on the infamous Varna Road in Balsal Heath which was a well-known red light area, and unless they have pulled it down since, I have no doubt it will still be infamous.

After walking for five minutes we turned off Varna Road with Pat leading the way. Suddenly, we could hear a little music as a door opened, and then seemed to close, cutting off the music once again.

It suddenly clicked where he was taking me, it was something that I had heard about a couple of times but had never been in one, I think they called them Shabbeens – the new craze that had started in Birmingham, (illegal cellar bars that were open all night).

The police knew all about them but for some reason left them alone. I was later told that they got a lot of information from their snouts that used the places to collect information for them, plus they were only in the very rough areas where the average person wouldn't go. By the way that was to be the first and last time! that I ever went into one.

By this time I had sobered up at least to the level at which I was in charge of my faculties, but never the less I was still a little bit wary of the people we would meet inside.

Since getting out of the Taxi Pat had said very little, and even concerning my questions of 'Where the fuck are you taking me? the only answer was a well-known remark where the Irish were concerned, 'Ah. Bejasus, Charlie! We'll be there in a minute' There wasn't a lot I could say to that.

When he managed to find where the place was, we had to descend at least a dozen steep steps and ring a bell. This was immediately followed by the opening of a small shutter that was fixed into the door at shoulder height' at the same time a very dim light came on, and a voice that sounded like that of a Jamaican, asked for our name. When

Pat gave him his full name, there was a roar of laughter accompanied by the words, 'So you've come to see me at last, you fucking latchigo!' and the door swung open.

As we stepped through, a very large Jamaican-grabbed hold of him like a long lost brother, while at the same time shouting to another of his countrymen working behind what seemed to be a makeshift bar, 'George! The Beers and anything else that these Lads fancy tonight are on the Fucking House!

After a minute or two of back slapping between Pat and his mate, we ended up at the bar, got our drinks and were able to look around, now that our eyes had become accustomed to the lack of light in the place.

The floor area was massive with lots of small archways leading off to other areas that you couldn't see without walking around to look for yourself. By the way they only served Bottled Beer, and always without a glass.

My first impression on entering the bar was that it didn't have a lot of customers' but after Pat and I had spent a few minutes walking around in and out of the archways and alcoves, I soon changed my mind.

There must have been fifty people or more. There were some sat at tables playing cards with piles of money in front of them. I later found out they were playing three-card brag, and it certainly wasn't for pennies. There were men dressed up as women, but in that light I wouldn't have known that they weren't women if Pat hadn't told me. In one of the alcoves, there were half a dozen well-dressed couples. Some of the men were obviously the older well-off type with some of them dressed in expensive suits. As I looked closer, I could see one or two hands disappearing under the girls' short skirts with a bit of moaning and groaning accompanying them' on hearing these sounds my Dick immediately began to rise!

We managed to find a table in the corner of one of the alcoves, and settled down to drink our beer, and I began to question Pat about the place he had brought me to, which I was beginning to enjoy. "The atmosphere was now beginning to feel fantastic"

Apparently the two Jamaicans were brothers and over the past couple of years had done a lot of casual work for Pat and his brother, they were great workers and easy-going. Over a period of time, Pat, more so than his brother, who I later found to be a bit of a miserable Bastard, had become good mates with his workers, to the point of sometimes meeting socially as in family-wise, it was while he was telling me all this that George the barman brought us another drink on the house and told us to get it down our necks, that there was plenty more where that had come from. By this time I was really getting into it in a big way, and of course a little drunker.

It was while Pat was in the bogs that a nice looking young girl not much older than myself sat down at our table, and introduced herself. She was from Liverpool, not that she had to tell me that, as I knew it the moment she opened her mouth. When I asked her what a nice girl like her was doing in this Den of iniquity, she burst out laughing, but before she could answer Pat had returned to the table with another two Beers.

After introductions she started to give us her story; she was a prostitute and had been in the profession for the past two years, despite being aged 18 at the time of telling us her story.

She told us that most of her clients were in their 50s, and older, with the majority of them preferring young girls, in fact the younger the better, and that a lot of them treated her like a naughty daughter or niece. She then started to tell us about some of her experiences and in no time she had us roaring our heads off' She was hilarious! I realized later in life, after meeting and working with Liverpool lads, that part of their make-up is to make a joke out of any situation, good or bad, and that this was just one of their many gifts. She then changed the subject and started to tell us why she had decided to become a prostitute. She had been born in Liverpool and was just one of ten kids' and like myself and many others, she had been brought up on the breadline, her mother being worn out by 30 and her father being unemployed for as long as she could remember. By the age of 13, one of her uncle's had seduced her which she admitted to us she had thoroughly enjoyed and would probably have seduced him beforehand if she had realized what having sex was like.

She carried on her affair with her uncle until she was sixteen but had been with many other men while the affair was going on.

Just before her sixteenth birthday, after weighing up her future, and speaking to one of her girlfriends who was already selling herself and making good money, she decided that she would leave Liverpool, move to Birmingham where no one knew her and become a prostitute for five years – and not a minute longer!

She knew that after that amount of time she would be able to return to Liverpool with plenty of money in the bank, buy her own house, start her own business if she wished, and settle down with some nice man, preferably a few years older than herself, who would look after her.

By the time she had finished her story, I had a lob on, especially after some of the scenes she had described to us. Then, out of the blue, she said, taking hold of my hand, 'Come on Charlie' it's time to go!

Before I had realized what was going on I had said to her, 'Not with me love' I have never paid for it in my life, and I am not going to start now! Try my mate!

With this, Pat burst out laughing. 'Don't worry about it, Charlie! It's a belated birthday present on the house, so get on with it, and I'll have a chat with my mate while you're doing your thing.'

The House stairs led out of the cellar where she had a nice comfortable room on the first floor. When we entered she turned to me with a smile on her face, and told me that I was the first virgin she had ever had, and she was going to give me a real good time.

If Pat had been in the room with us at that time I would have choked him, but as it happened she had already got my trousers around my ankles and beginning to stroke my already half-erect penis. As soon as it was hard, she slid a Durex onto it, pulled her skirt up to her waist, told me to step out of my trousers and commenced to pull me down on to the bed beside her, at the same time telling me to relax and enjoy my first time.

All the time that she was talking, she was pumping my cock up and down, keeping it hard, not that she needed to. I had now forgotten my previous embarrassment and was raring to go. All of a sudden she was sat on my stomach, then lifting her thighs off the bed she slipped my cock into her hole. I was mesmerized at seeing my hard cock being guided, for the first time in its young life, by this young girl's hand through her forest of hair and into the now visible pink lips between her legs, and I will always remember those pink lips on either side of my cock as it passed into her body. I must have fucked her for twenty minutes or more before exploding in the Durex.

Up until then, I had always thought that prostitutes didn't have an orgasm while they were with a punter. If so, I can only say that where this young lady was concerned, if that wasn't an orgasm I had felt inside her, then she must have been a brilliant actress as well as a terrific ride. Happy birthday! And Cheers, Pat!

After my birthday present from Pat I didn't see him again for a few weeks. When I did he was in the company of my brother Sean, and it was obvious to me that he had kept his promise' that he would never tell anyone that I had been down Varna Road to lose my virginity.

My First Love

It wasn't to be long after my escapade with him that I met a lovely looking young girl, the quiet type, who I fell for right away – lock, stock and barrel. Her name was Mary and I met her through her father, a local rag and bone man called Harry who also happened to be one of the local characters, and a well-known story teller.

I met him in the Bishopgate pub one Saturday night when I called in to buy Melia a couple of halves. As it happened, he and Melia were good friends and had been so for many years.

While I was sitting with her, he came over and sat at our table' that was when she introduced us to one another. Harry and I got on like a house on fire and by the end of the night; all three of us were as pissed as newts.

A few weeks later I bumped into him again pushing his rag and bone cart; I think it was one of the very few days that I had skived off work.

It was coming up to dinnertime' and Harry had just weighed in his tat at the local scrap yard' and on seeing me' invited me in for a drink at his then local, the Roebuck on Broad Street, for a couple of pints, and a bit of a laugh.

At throwing-out time, he talked me into going to his house for a sandwich and a cup of tea. That was the first time I set eyes on his daughter Mary, who ignored me completely.

Council Housing

I would just like to take a minute two to give you an idea of some of the characteristics of the area where Harry lived along with some of the amenities supplied to the tenants by their landlord, the Birmingham City Council.

On each side of the street you had a row of old terraced houses which would stretch from one corner of the street to the other, and on each corner was either a pub or a corner shop, but along this particular stretch of terraced houses were archways, every three or four houses, that led you through to what I can only describe as an enclosed cobbled courtyard, each of which contained a small row of terraced properties that were normally built at right angles to the rear walls of the Arch wayed terraced houses that you entered through. They were called entries in those days!

In front of these small two bedroomed terraced properties, 10 yards away, was a line of wash houses, each one shared by two families, and inside each of them was a large, cast-iron pot built into a table of brickwork, with an iron-type fire in place directly beneath the iron it where you put your wood to boil your water. The top was finished off with a wooden scrubbing board, on top of which was a cast iron mangle.

Can you just imagine the young Women of today having to do that kind of work to supply their kids with clean clothes? They would all end up running around like a load of scruffs!

At the rear of the same properties was a row of toilets, one for each property, and on entering one you would invariably find a nail sticking out of the wall with small squares of newspaper stuck on it' but only in the posh ones' in the remainder you would find old newspapers either stuck behind the loo pipe that ran down the wall' or thrown over the toilet floor' but there was one thing that they all had in common! After wiping your Arse with a few pieces of that newspaper, whether on the nail or the floor' you ended up not only with a sore Arse' but a black one to boot!

Getting back to Harry and his lovely daughter, who was soon to be the first real love of my life, and the only one I would never forget. Then again, I do believe that the majority – male and female, normally remember the first one.

Anyway on that occasion she completely ignored me, so much so that she didn't even acknowledge me when I walked into her house' and likewise when I was leaving' so of course I automatically assumed that she wasn't interested.

Harry had three other kids, all boys, with Pete being the eldest and of a similar character to his old Man.

It must have been two or three weeks after meeting Mary that I bumped into him walking down the road with his young girlfriend.

While we were having a chat, he asked why I hadn't been around to the house as his sister had been asking after me, in fact he reckoned she fancied me.

A few days later, I called at their house to see if Harry was going for a couple of beers and his daughter Mary actually said hello to me' and believe it or not she actually had a smile on her face.

Her dad and I decided to go on a pub crawl along Broad Street where there were three or four pubs he was well known in, and we ended up having a real good night. I think in all the times I went on the Beer with him, there wasn't one time when I didn't enjoy his company' and sense of humor.

Another thing I found when in the company of Harry was that I was beginning to make a lot more friends, and also getting to know a lot more of what was going down in the area.

Over the next two or three weeks, apart from having the odd Beer with him, I began calling at the house to see how he was doing as an excuse for seeing and chatting to Mary, and the more I went to her house the friendlier she became. I eventually plucked up the courage to ask her out to the local picture house. Unlike today, young girls were frowned on if they went into a pub' and on reflection, to say it was a man's world in those days is putting it mildly.

The only women who seemed to be accepted in pubs were normally wives accompanied by their husbands, old women, and those on the game, who were women normally in their late Twenties to early Thirties.

So invariably courting couples normally ended up in the back rows of the local picture house; (normally referred to as the local flea Pit) which was always the darkest area in the House and the one where the usherette had the least chance of catching you fondling each other.

Anyway, back to the back row, and getting the Show on the road. No doubt most of you will know the procedure, having, on the law of averages, been in the same situation yourselves in some way or another.

The normal way to start the ball rolling was with a bit of smooching, as in kissing – by the way, no tongues in those days, more's the pity' if there had been we could have got the girls going a lot quicker. As it was, you were lucky to get them half-going by throwing out time, which I suppose wasn't that bad providing you had, or knew off, an alleyway or similar on the way home where hopefully you would manage to finish her off, or at the very least have a 'J. Arthur. Rank' as consolation prize.

Sitting on the back seats with Mary' which I had envisaged on numerous occasions, didn't turn out quite the same in reality. It must have taken me at least half an hour to put my arm over the seat and give her a kiss, and I would swear to this day that she had never kissed a boy before that moment in time.

Never the less, as we have all had to do at some time in our lives I persevered and by throwing-out time she had allowed me to feel her breasts' and, my God, the struggle had been worth it! She had lovely tits, but try as I might, I couldn't persuade her to stroke my hard on, not even over the outside of my trousers, and I knew then that I had a virgin, and she would be a hard nut to crack, but at least I had broken the ice. Ride on Sir Galahad! Or was it 'Into the Valley of Death rode the six hundred!' Only time would tell.

Over the next few weeks I took her out on several occasions and apart from the pictures, the only other place to take her were for strolls along the canal bank where I eventually got her to the point' where she would let me play with her lovely tits! However, more often than not she would only let me undo her Bra at the back so I could do it up quickly if someone came along.

It was around the same time that I had started courting Mary that I made friends with a lad called Tommy Mack who I had spoken to once or twice in the local pubs.

One Saturday night after I had had two or three pints in the Roebuck, on the corner of Broad Street and Ledsam Street, I began to make my way home via Bishopsgate Street where part of my route led across a piece of wasteland, that had been bombed in the war' and later cleared of the rubble. I was about halfway across when I made out the figure of Tommy Mack. He was on the ground, and two fella's were kicking the shit out of him.

One thing beer always did for me was to get rid of my inhibitions' and without thinking, I nutted one of the lads on the nose and he went down, and I commenced to put the boot in. By this time, with the pressure off him, Tommy was back on his feet, had managed to deck the other lad and commenced to do to him the same as I was doing to his mate! After a few boots they had had enough, and scarpered.

After having a quick look at him, I saw that he wasn't as badly beaten as I had first thought' so I said goodnight and headed for home. When I awoke the following morning, I began to wonder if Tommy was all right.

Sunday lunchtime drinking hours were always twelve o'clock until two and I would normally go to my (then) main local, the Victoria inn' which was near enough to the area' where I thought Tommy lived.

After asking around in the area, someone directed me to the White Horse, where he assured me I would find him in the back room playing dominoes. As it happened, he was standing at the bar having a beer with a couple of bruises showing on his face and, as I was to find out later, a good many on his body.

We ended up having a right good session; in fact by closing time we were pissed out of our heads, and from then on we became the best of mates.

CHAPTER 5

At that time in our Great Countries Character' every small area around Birmingham centre had its own gang, and every now and then they would encroach on one another's patch.

It was on such a weekend when a crowd of us had had a few drinks that one of the lads suggested that for a change it would be nice to go and have a drink in another gangs Area' on the off chance of picking up some crumpet, and also knowing that there was a fair chance that by the end of the night there would be some aggro. It was on that night that I came unstuck.

We had had a great night, and as usual the lads drifted apart, going their separate ways. Tommy Mack and I decided to have a walk into Birmingham town centre where there were lots of all night coffee bars, and plenty of girls knocking about. After ordering two coffees, we sat down opposite two young girls who looked to be on their own, and started to chat them up.

The one I sat facing was a little beauty with what looked to be a nice pair of 'Bristol Cities' and at that time in my life I was definitely into those. I sometimes thought, in later years, that this feeling that I had for big tits stemmed from the fact that when I was a baby I didn't have much of a sucking time!

The one Tommy was facing was a plump girl. By the way, have you ever noticed, even in this day and age when you see a couple of girls out shopping, or in a pub, there is always a smart one that you wouldn't mind giving one to, and an ugly one who you wouldn't even consider lending one to! Tommy's was one of those!

While he was chatting her up you could see she was playing hard to get. Incidentally, have you ever noticed that the uglier they are, the harder it is to get into their knickers? And from where I was sitting it looked to me as though Tommy was fighting a losing battle with this extra large pair!

I on the other hand, was doing quite well. In fact I had got to the point where I thought I had cracked it, but unbeknown to me, things were about to change, and as it turned out it wasn't to be for the better. Out of the blue, three lads appeared at our table and started slagging the girls off.

Apparently, or so it seemed, the good-looking one was one of the lads' ex-girlfriends and they hadn't parted on the best of terms. It was probably due to the fact that he had caught his best mate stuck up her you-know-what in an alleyway' near to where she lived.

Talk about rubbing salt into his wounds! It happened twenty minutes after he had seen her home to her front door, after having taken her out for the night. Alas, as they normally did after a night out, they ended up in the same alleyway which they had used regularly, where he had as usual expected to have his leg-over, but it turned out that she wasn't having any of it, as she wasn't feeling well.

Put yourself, for a moment, in the same situation as this lad found himself ! After having a cup of coffee, he was on his way home, which brought him past his favourite alleyway where, lo and behold, he found his best mate going ten to the dozen with his sick girlfriend, who now had her legs wrapped around his mate's waist, squealing her head off as she rammed herself up and down on his rather large manhood. Needless to say, her boyfriend who thought a lot of her – lost his marbles and smashed his fist into the side of what used to be his best mate's head, and on doing so, stopped both his girl and his best mate from coming their cocoa!

The last time he had seen his now ex-girlfriend was when she was running down the road screaming and trying to pull her knickers up over her bare Arse at the same time. By the way, it was to be much later that he told me this story.

Back in the coffee house, at that particular moment, all I was after was to give her the same as his best mate had given her, with bells on. Never the less, we now found ourselves in a very dodgy position. Just think about it for a minute, there's me and Tommy sat down in a cubicle that I couldn't get out of unless Tommy moved. On top of that, we had these three lads standing over us blocking our escape and threatening to give us a right good kicking.

To cut a long story short, Tommy did the only thing he could under the circumstances. He picked the table up and threw it at them, coffee and all. At the same time, I jumped up and butted one of them. Then all hell broke loose, and they commenced to knock the shit out of us! The next thing I knew we were in the back of a police van on our way to Steelhouse Lane police station where we all spent the rest of the night as guests of Her Majesty's Government.

Her Majesty's Pleasure

At ten o'clock the following morning we appeared in court where Tommy and the three lads were given bail for seven days and I was remanded for the same amount of time in Winson Green prison, mainly because I wasn't living with my old man and therefore they looked on me as possibly doing a disappearing act. In retrospect, they were probably right.

A week later the five of us appeared in court for sentencing. Tommy and two of the lads got probation, Tommy mainly because he had health problems, and had a letter from his doctor verifying it. It came as a bit of a surprise to me as I had no idea he suffered with this problem. The other lad and I received three months in what they call nowadays a detention centre, because we had the worst criminal records out of the five.

When we arrived at our destination in Berkshire we found it wasn't as bad as we had been led to believe, I think the worst part of it was having to get up at five o'clock in the morning and do a three mile cross country run before breakfast; it certainly gave us a good appetite!

The centre was run on the lines of doing your National Service, probably with the idea that a person's time wouldn't be wasted in there, even more so as a lot of the inmates would be eligible for call up on or just after their release. Needless to say everything was done at the double, which I think also applied to taking a piss. Apart from that, it was okay.

The lad I had come in with' like myself was called Charlie and believe it or not we became good mates. When you think back to the first time we met, kicking the shit out of one another, it was a good do!

I had only ever seen Charlie drunk, the once, and as to being a hooligan and as hard as nails could not be denied but as a sober person, he was the opposite. In fact, he could make friends with anyone, and was always the heart and soul of the party in our recreation time, which needless to say there was very little off.

On my day of release, my old mate Tommy was waiting outside for me along with one of Charlie's mates, who was one of the original ones who had been given probation.

The four of us ended up in the nearest pub, and commenced' to getting pissed out of our minds.

When we arrived back in Brum, Tommy gave me a few quid to keep me going until I found some work. By the way you didn't have social workers and do-gooders waiting for you, in readiness to wipe your fucking Arse, and tell you that your problem wasn't really of your making, but the fault of the system.

***

Once again I moved into my bed-sit on Wheeleys Road with my old schoolmate Johnny, who had some bad news for me. My girlfriend Mary, who I adored, had become pregnant and married someone else, and to make things worse, it was someone that I knew.

All this had happened because I went into town for a coffee, nearly had my leg-over, got beaten up and ended up in Winston Green Prison, followed by three months in a detention centre. Have you ever had the feeling that some bastard! Up there doesn't like you? I certainly did at that moment in time!

It was a few weeks later that I bumped into Mary's dad, who was almost as sick as I was about what had happened.

At the time she had started seeing the other lad, she had been told by someone that I had been sent down for twelve months, and she didn't know whether I would come back to the area or not.

As always, life carries on, and Tommy and I started to pull the girls on a regular basis, and my sex life was great, even so for a long time Mary was never far from my mind, and I vowed to myself never to put myself in that position again with another girl.

Shortly after my release I met another lad named Thomas, nicknamed 'Knocker' Thomas, in a pub called the

Albion, which Tommy and I had started to use on Friday nights for a game of dominoes. The same pub was also known as the best pint of beer in the surrounding area; another added attraction was being able to have a pint with my eldest brother Jack who used the same pub most weekends.

Getting back to Knocker, he was one of those who, when out on the town, was always immaculately dressed, with normally not a hair out of place, I bet you've guessed already – yes, he certainly was a ladies' man, and well known for it.

He stood around five foot eight in height and was of a slim build, fairly good looking in a rugged kind of way, had jet-black hair in the style of the day, a Tony Curtis at the front and what they called, in those days, a duck's arse at the back. To finish it off, he was always good company to be in.

Tommy's and my normal routine on a Friday night consisted of having a couple of pints, a game of dominoes, and then head off down the road to the Railway Club, which was five minutes walk from the Albion' where every weekend they had a rock'n'roll band, which attracted a lot of young ladies.

It was on one of these nights that Knocker mentioned there was a girl he really fancied, but she was always in the company of two other girls, and asked us if we would help split them up, so he could have his evil way with her.

After about an hour of chatting them up and buying them drinks, with a bit of rock'n'roll in between they became quite friendly, and agreed to let us walk them home at closing time, which obviously made Knocker very happy. Not Tommy though, he had ended up with the ugliest one! It was only after Knocker agreeing to buy mine and Tommy's beer the following dinner time that Tommy agreed to take the ugly one home.

As it happened, all three girls lived in the Ledsam Street area which wasn't quite as rough as the area's we lived in. In retrospect I think at that particular time, and because of where they lived, they thought they were a bit above us, especially the ugly one.

To get to that area you had to pass a well known courting spot called Canal Street, which was infact opposite the Albion pub that we had been in earlier in the evening.

Canal Street was only four or five hundred yards in length, at the end of which was a gateway entrance into the canal area. Needless to say, the courting couples of the day used it on a regular basis. It had, on both sides of the street, what I can only describe as large factory gates with three foot recesses where no one could see you without actually passing the spot you were in; it was certainly a first class place to have a shag!.

As the three of us left the club the girl I was with and myself ended up a few yards behind the other four. By this time, the lady in question had become very friendly to the point that we were necking on and off on our way up the road which put the others, by the time we approached Canal Street, thirty or forty yards in front of us.

At the entrance to Canal Street my girl and I disappeared into it, and about halfway down found ourselves a well recessed doorway.

To say she was getting into the mood would be an understatement' and I felt sure that with a bit of pushing I just might get into her knickers. Ten minutes after entering our doorway I achieved my goal; my fingers were playing with her vagina on the outside of her knickers. I had cracked it, or so I thought. She, by this time, had my penis out of my trousers and was giving it a good hand job.

All of a sudden she pushed my hand away from her Fanny, no sooner had she done this' than she immediately slipped down the wall and put her lips around my now throbbing knob-end! You can imagine the surprise I received with this action, coming out of the blue like it had. The moment her soft lips touched my cock I ejaculated, she was obviously used to doing this, as she whipped my cock out of her mouth as it started to spurt!
That was the first time a girl had ever done that to me, but I am happy to say' it wasn't to be the last.

The next time I took her out, which I did on numerous occasions, she told me that she had been sucking her boyfriend's penis for the last twelve months or more' and that seemed to have had something to do with her having been a virgin until recently. Apparently her boyfriend loved his cock sucked so much, that he didn't bother where getting between her legs was concerned, but you can rest assured I made up for that in the months ahead.

When I met Tommy and Knocker at the Swan on Grosvenor Street the following day, it turned out that Knocker's girl was a virgin and he had to settle for a 'ham shank'. On the other hand, Tommy had walked his girl home to her front door, given her a kiss on the cheek and went home, so you can imagine the cost of the beer where that dinner time session was concerned, and all paid for by Knocker. Even I managed to get a couple of free ones. After all, I had helped him out as well as Tommy' and I truly believe where Knocker was concerned that' that dinner time session will go down as the most expensive 'ham shank' he was ever likely to have.

Pam was the name of the girl I took down Albion Street' and I had arranged to meet her one night the following week when she wasn't seeing her boyfriend, the meeting was to take place at the Bulls Head, another pub on Bishopsgate Street.

She looked good enough to eat as she walked into the lounge bar. After a couple of beers we were totally relaxed with one another, and I was happy to see she had a good sense of humour.

After a couple more beers I invited her down to my bed-sit. By the way, unlike the first time we met, I now knew for certain that she would drop them!

I would like to take a minute to introduce you to my new girlfriend, part-time of course, she was slightly over five foot in height, with a lovely, slim figure, and she had the most beautiful little arse I had come across since my ex-girlfriend had dumped me.

To make it even better she had lovely breasts, the type where the nipples turn up on the ends, Body wise she was lovely. The only thing that stopped her from being a raving beauty was her looks which you would class as attractive but in an average sort of way. On top of that she was a very open and friendly person, who seemed kind-natured and with a good sense of humour, which is a trait that you rarely find in many women today.

When we arrived at the bed-sit we lost no time in getting down to the nitty-gritty, but I had a problem trying to get her to strip off completely, as up to then she hadn't even done so for her boyfriend. With a little bit of coaxing and a few strokes of her superb breasts, she agreed, but only if I would close my eyes until she got under the bedclothes, which of course I readily agreed to do.

By this time I was naked myself, and to say I had a hard-on is an understatement. My penis was so hard that it was hurting and badly needed to go somewhere quickly for a bit of relief.

After a bit of sex play, I got between her lovely legs, and it didn't take me long to get her lubricated and panting a little. Nevertheless, I had a bloody hard time getting into her; she was as tight as a drum. In fact, if my cock had been any softer I would never have gained entry. As it was, by the time my dick was fully embedded in her I was nearly ready for pumping and the squeals coming out of her were nobody's business, except for the fact that they turned me on so much that I couldn't hold back any longer and gave her the full caboodle, balls and all.

My God, she was tight! In fact she was probably tighter than any Scotsman I have ever had the misfortune to meet, and believe you me, I have met plenty.

Pam was meeting her boyfriend at eleven o'clock but by the time we had finished, I must have fucked her three or four times, and would probably have given her some more, which I am sure she would have enjoyed' although I don't think she had realized until then, just how much she loved it' and I also believe that she later cut her boyfriend's cock-sucking sessions down until he had used that tight little hole between her legs.

My affair with Pam had certainly turned out to be the start of a beautiful friendship that was to last for many months to come, and she was to later tell me it was the best time she had ever had. (I am still not sure if she was referring to the cock or the company)

The Beatniks

It was during one of our pub crawls that we met Micky Smith. In those days if you wanted to go incognito you would call yourself Smith, so invariably when he introduced himself he would receive a bit of a smile or a funny look.

Over a short period of time we became good friends' and now and then while out on the beer, Tommy, Micky and myself would get up and take off the Everley Brothers. So what happens after a while? They would call us the the fucking Everleys every time we walked into a pub. People would go to any lengths in those days to find an excuse to take the piss out of you, even your best friends.

Most of the clientele who used these pubs were what you would call Irish Brummies, which meant of course that they were the off springs of Irish parents, but had actually been born in England. Nevertheless, they retained their parents' love for Irish music' such as Kevin Barry, 'Dirty Old Town', the 'Irish Rover' etc. Normally, by the end of most nights at the weekend we would end up singing these kind of songs, but alas as in any pub – but possibly more so in Irish orientated ones – there were always a fair few fisticuffs flaring up and the way the landlord dealt with them was to throw the people going at it into the backyard of the pub. They all had one in those days, and the people fighting were not allowed in again until they had settled their differences. This way the pubs rarely received any damage to their interiors.

Micky Smith was the first mate I had ever had who you could call educated and talked without a Brummie accent, but nevertheless, the lads accepted him, I think mainly for the fact that he loved Irish music and knew more Irish songs than the rest of them put together.

He was also one of those people who we classed as a good patter merchant. His patter of course specialised solely, where the pulling of women was concerned' and with these credentials to his name, who couldn't help but like him? It was just after meeting him that the beatniks started to come on the scene in a big way and quite a lot of these were dropouts from colleges and universities, with the majority of them taking over large empty houses and squatting. These were mainly in the Hagley Road area of Edgbaston which was a well known upper-class area.

One particular evening sticks in my mind to this day! When for a change to our normal routine we decided to go into town for a night out in good old Yates's Wine Lodge . I'm not sure now, but I think it was on a Friday evening, and at that time in our country's history, the Wine Lodge was situated on Corporation Street' in the city centre' and was purported to have the longest bar in Europe. On top of that, the wine, beer and shorts were a lot cheaper than your local pubs.

To enter Yates's, you had to walk up half a dozen steps into what looked like, in those days, to be the foyer of a picture house. From there, if you wanted beer or wine you would then walk through a pair of double doors, directly in front of you, where you would find an enormous bar running the full length of the left-hand wall' at the end of which there was an exit to the road behind. The whole of the ground floor had the appearance of a large, somewhat fancy, barn with sawdust on the floor and old brass spittoons scattered around.

If you happened to be into Whisky, or any other kind of shorts for that matter, you would have to walk up a rather large flight of stairs to a somewhat smaller bar.

We made our choice and headed upstairs where we had a couple of shorts, then descended to the main bar on the ground floor, and started on the wine. Australian white was the drink of the day' and after a couple of these down our necks, Micky started to talk to a crowd of beatniks.

There were plenty of girls amongst them with some of them being quite good looking, and I did notice that the more wine I drank, the better looking they became.

It was also very easy to see by the looks of some of them, that they hadn't washed in weeks, but that wouldn't deter us from giving them one, if the opportunity arose.

We were on our third wine' when John introduced Tommy and me to what had now become his and our company for the rest of the night, hopefully all night!

At closing time they invited us to their squat, which turned out to be a very large house just off Hagley Road, untenanted of course, and standing in its own grounds, which there looked to be plenty of.

When we entered the house, I could see right away that once upon a time it must have been' and probably still was, owned by one of our rich fraternity. The ground floor consisted of a very large entrance with a winding staircase running off to the left of it' added to this was half a dozen large rooms on the ground floor' and It was easy for anyone to see that once upon a time it had been a beautiful property, and no doubt with a lot of money spent on it, could be so again.

Most of the ground floor rooms were being used by the beatniks, and were mainly taken up by old settees and sleeping bags, along with the numerous empty beer bottles, fish and chip papers, baked bean cans and numerous other items off refuse.

Overall I would have deemed it as being more than suitable for the local rats to do their breeding' and by the looks of things' there was every possibility that we had now found ourselves in the company of some of them.

After settling down on one of the many settees in attendance' along with a bottle of beer and a bit of music from an old clapped out wireless' I began to relax.

We had been in the place for less than twenty minutes when it began to open up. It started with one of the girls producing a few roll-ups of marijuana which she began to pass around' ten minutes later I looked around for my mates and on seeing them it was obvious that they had already helped themselves to a couple of puffs' and looked to be well on their travels' added to this was the girls now wandering around kissing everyone' and my friends, the atmosphere was way out' and I hadn't even had a Puff!
In the past, I had tried pot on one or two occasions but the only effect it had on my system was heartburn so needless to say I stuck to the beer and the girls, in that order, the girls coming a very close second!

Some of you will know, but for those who don't I will try to explain – more or less, the effect it normally has on someone who is susceptible to it, after two or three puffs it gives them a very clear, languid mind, totally relaxing' exterminates all inhibitions and makes you, in a lot of cases, love everyone.

Most of the girls were between sixteen and twenty years of age, and thank God, they were full of it. They were all shapes and sizes, and once again Tommy drew the attention of a little plump girl who, in no time at all, had his cock out and was sucking it as though it was a long lost friend. However, unlike previous times where plump girls had been concerned, and given Tommy's dislike of them, there is no doubt in my mind that it was the pot' and that alone! that had sorted him out where his inhibitions were concerned' as he now laid back' and thoroughly enjoyed her attentions.

Micky, on the other hand, was stripped off and lying in a corner on top of a sleeping bag, stuck up a little beauty, and was oblivious to anything else. In fact, I think you could have pissed on him and he wouldn't have noticed!
By this time, most of the women were totally naked and, as I was to find out later, if you were invited to a beatniks' commune, and providing the girl in question liked you, you could fuck her all night, along with the boyfriend's blessing. Mind you, sometimes I believe the boyfriend would join in and when his cock was hard he was inclined not to bother whose hole he stuck it in! Just as long as it went somewhere, so in future beware! Mind you, if the pot totally got rid of your inhibitions, who knows, you might enjoy it. God help us all! In the past I had rarely seen Tommy performing, but that night he was full of it, and made quite sure that the girls got it all! lock, cock and barrel.

A New World

It was shortly after the beatniks' party that I got a new job as a pipe fitter's mate, working out of town. The money was good and they paid for your lodgings, which was a bonus where I was concerned.

The first place they sent me to' was Nottingham, working on a new heating system at the main cinema on Angel Row which was situated in the town centre, where my main job consisted of cutting steel pipes, and screwing threads on them, it was bloody hard work.

There were six of us on the job, three fitters and three mates, and invariably three or four of us would be out most nights on the beer, and seeing what we could pick up.

The other two fitters' mates were from Liverpool and we got on like a house on fire. In the centre of town was Yates's Wine Lodge' it was a lovely place and by far the smartest one that I had been in up until then. As you entered the front door, there was a beautiful old-fashioned polished wooden bar on the left-hand side. There were large chandeliers hanging from the ceilings, the floors were polished pine' and to top it off, there was a balcony in the same pine circling the whole bar. After ordering three beers we decided to explore it further. When we arrived upstairs, drinks in hand, there was an old chap wearing coat tails and a bow tie seated at a grand piano playing classical music. Needless to say, the atmosphere was one on its own! And from that night onwards we used the place more or less as our local (if we had nothing else to do)

The Characteristics Of Nottingham In The 60's

At that particular time, and quite possibly to this day, the women outnumbered the men by two to one, and that was according to the official Government census, so on that alone we knew we were going to have a good time. To top it off, we also earned much more money than the local male population, so were always able to spend freely on the ladies.

There was also a downside to Nottingham. It had the largest percentage of venereal disease in the United Kingdom, and that was official! But like everything else, when you're young you think it won't happen to you and, anyway, you will be right careful.

That kind of thinking is all right until you have had a few beers, and you're up an alley with a nice looking young lady! Your Cock is standing to attention, and you know that time is of the essence' and that if you don't get in to her right away, she might change her mind!

Let's just think about this for a moment. There you are with a lob on and the young lady is panting for it, hopefully! you are now, looking for your Durex after supping eight or nine pints of beer. The law of averages is' you will never find your Durex, and if you manage to in the state you're in, your lob will have gone, your girl will have stopped panting' and you're up the fucking Swannie mate! So there you have it, in a nutshell.

Getting back to booze and women; most evenings the two Scousers and myself would do a tour of the local pubs' where after a while, we made the occasional friend.

On one such night we were chatting with a local lad, and having a right good craic with him' when out of the blue, he mentioned that he knew a good pub on the outskirts where there was live music and plenty of women.

When we arrived at the pub it was heaving and as usual we started chatting up the ladies. There were three of them together. One of them looked to be quite young, maybe sixteen or seventeen, one was in her early twenties and the other her early thirties.

I noticed right away that the young one and the older one favoured one another' this as we were to find out later was because they were mother and daughter.

After buying them a few drinks, they became quite friendly towards us, and we eventually got them to part with their names. The mother and daughter were called Mary and Ann and their friend was called Sue.

At throwing out time Sue was picked up by her boyfriend, and the new friend who had brought us to the pub had to leave as he had an early start the next day. That, of course, left us three, and mother and daughter, who to our surprise invited us to their flat for a quick drink.

When the taxi reached their flat, we had quite a shock! it was in the expensive part of town' and on entering' it was absolutely gorgeous; it was in fact the kind of place where you would automatically want to take your shoes off before entering.

While the ladies were sorting the drinks out I began to think how the fuck' could these two lovely young women afford a flat like the one we were now sitting in' the first thought that came to mind was that they must be on the game, and had picked us up' after seeing us throwing our money around! As we were to find out later, nothing could have been further from the truth.

Less than ten minutes after we arrived' there was soft music' and we had settled down on plush settees' along with our drinks' and started chatting to the girls.

It didn't take long for us to find out that the mother had some kind of escort agency, and we were even more surprised when she told us' that she was also part-owner of two or three nightclubs, so they were in fact quite wealthy young women, which started me wondering what the fuck they were doing bringing home three Arseholes like us. It wasn't to be long before we found out why – the mother was in to young lads in the 16 to 25 age bracket, and the daughter helped her pull them!

After twenty minutes of chat I excused myself because of the need to use the toilet. On my way back I bumped into the daughter and we started kissing. At the same time, she went straight for my Penis through my trousers and within a couple of minutes she had dragged me into a bedroom. By this time my hand was already under her bra, and grasping her small hard tits, and In no time at all we were both panting' and bollock naked! I had just got to where I was nibbling her nipples with my teeth' while grasping and massaging the cheeks of her firm little arse when one of my mates walked in on us, which to my surprise didn't seem to bother Mary who by now, was well on her way to getting off.

At the time I didn't realize' that the effect on her when my mate came in had tipped her over the edge' to her first orgasm of the night.

In no time at all, he was stripped off and on the bed, two minutes later she had taken his then rampant Penis between her soft lips, my own hands at the same time having begun to grasp and twist her extended nipples!

To say she was really going for it' is an understatement so much so' that she had now grasped the swollen head of my penis in her hand and began' in a somewhat aggressive way to drag it between the now wet lips of her vagina.

I had just slipped into her when my mate tried pushing me off, obviously having wanted to be first, but he was just a bit too late as by this time I was fully embedded' and going at her ten to the dozen. It wasn't long before we both got to where we were going, and at the same time my mate tried to unload himself into her mouth' but she wasn't having any of it! And immediately whipped it out of her mouth' its load splattering across her lovely breasts.

While we lay on the bed having a smoke, Mary made a hasty retreat to the bathroom to clean herself up' while mentioning on the way that she would bring us another drink just as soon as she had showered.

On finishing my cigarette I needed to go to the toilet, and decided on my way back to have a peep into the lounge to see how my other mate was doing with Mary's mother. As I entered the lounge, I couldn't believe what I was seeing. Ann, who was much smaller than my mate, was bent over the back of the settee with her feet at least six inches off the floor, while he, on the other hand, had hold of her by the top of her thighs and was driving his large penis in and out of her anus to the accompaniment of squeals coming from her beautiful mouth.

After watching this sight for less than thirty seconds, I was rock hard again and returned to Mary, my mind filled with the vision of that large cock going in and out of her Mothers lovely arse. As I entered the bedroom, Ann was lowering herself onto my mate's erect penis, and soon had the full length of him inside her, while at the same time my mate was squeezing her young breasts with what seemed to me to be undue aggressiveness, which nevertheless seemed to bring noises out of Mary that sounded somewhere between pleasure and pain...with most of it sounding more like pleasure! In two seconds flat I was mounted behind her as she was riding my mate, and told her that I had just seen her mother with a cock in her arse' and I was going to do the same to her. Before she could answer, I had my middle finger inside her tight little Bum hole getting her ready' for the forthcoming invasion' whether she wanted it or not!

By this time she seemed to be in outer space squealing and panting, with numerous other noises emitting from her throat. I didn't give her any further warning' and with only a nod to my mate' I suddenly grasped her small Arse on one of her upward movements' and not allowing her to lower herself while at the same time with a hard push I began to force the swollen head of my penis into her now slightly lubricated entrance with as much force as I could muster, this action was immediately followed by two or three far louder squeals than I had heard up until then' and became even louder as I drove the full length into her, two minutes later I had been discharged'(3 stripes for good duty) this was followed half an hour later by my mate's cock doing likewise, and she loved every second of it. All I can add to this statement is God help the lad who marries her! He would need the stamina' and dick of a donkey' to sort lovely little Mary out.

It must have been around four in the morning when we left their flat, completely knackered.

We were in a right state when we arrived for work, the following day and needless to say it was another couple of nights before we were fit enough to hit the town again. Have you ever thought about when you were teenager, and how easy it was to get a lob on, and how you could perform three or four times a night, and still be up fit for work the next day? I don't know about you but when I manage to get a lob on nowadays, finished with the leg-over, I need my rocking chair for a week!

Back In Brum

The weekend following our meeting with the Mother and Daughter' my turn had come around for a free rail ticket home.

When I arrived in Birmingham my first stop was my bed-sit to drop off my gear and settle up any rent that I owed to my mate Jimmy. Then, as normal, after being out of town for a month I would take him up to his local pub and buy him a couple of pints before meeting Tommy Mack.

As it was Friday night, I knew where Tommy and Knocker would be, unless of course they had changed their habits in the past four weeks which I thought was pretty unlikely. When I arrived at the Albion there was no sign off them, or my Brother for that matter. Never the less, I had a pint of beer assuming it wouldn't be long before one of them would turn up.

By the time I had finished my second Beer there was still no sign off them, so I decided to take a walk up the road to the White Swan, as every now and then Tommy and I would call in there on our way down to the Albion. Sure enough, they were there in the smoke room having a beer with Cockney John, an old friend of Knocker's from way back. Tommy and I didn't know the Cockney very well as up until then we had only met him once or twice, and at those times he had always had his girl friend on his arm.

Cockney's girlfriend was a real beauty and never failed to turn heads wherever she went; but alas she was what we called, a stuck up cow!

The three of them were just drinking up' and we made our way to the Albion, while listening to the cockney's jokes. They were always a bit way out, I suppose nowadays you would call them sick jokes, about spastics, etc. No doubt you will know what I mean, but in those days probably because of the lack of education, people didn't see anything wrong in laughing at them, and especially the way the cockney told them. I suppose it helped the fact that he was always the life and soul of the party, and a very likeable fellow.

As usual, we had a couple of pints, had a chat with my brother Jack who by then had arrived with his mates' and headed down to the Railway Club. It was while we were at the bar that I noticed Pam' and just as I was about to raise my arm to her, a well-built young man sat down beside her with a couple of drinks, so that had definitely knocked it on the head for my leg-over, not that I was bothered too much, as for the past few days I had been feeling a bit under the weather, and had put it down to the session that I had had a few days previously with' mother and daughter.

We hadn't been in the club for more than ten minutes when Knocker's girlfriend turned up with one of her mates who, in no time, had fallen under the spell of the Cockney he had that effect on women' and the pair of them started dancing. It wasn't long before Knocker and his girlfriend joined them on the dance floor.

Knocker wasn't much off a dancer, and normally wouldn't bother, but with a bit of coaxing from his girlfriend, along with a few kisses had succumbed to her request. On the other hand, the Cockney could really swing it. In fact, he could do a good impression of Elvis, and it wasn't long before the other dancers had made a circle around him so they could watch him perform, followed of course by clapping and howling for more when he had finished.

It was shortly after the dancing spectacle that the Cockney had to leave in order to catch his last bus home. In those days, the buses stopped running at 11 o'clock and at the time he lived ten miles outside the town centre.

Until he disappeared we hadn't been able to talk about what had gone on while I had been away. It turned out that Knocker had carried on seeing the girl that he had met at the club four weeks earlier, and apparently after another two or three dates he had managed to get her to drop her knickers, and gave her a good seeing-to, and after a few more seeings-to, he was suddenly in love. I was a bit sick with this news. My God! What next? All I needed now was Tommy falling for the ugly one and I would have to start looking around for some new mates.

As these thoughts were going through my mind, Ugly was sat across the room making gooey eyes at him. Poor Tommy, we did give him some stick that night.

At closing time, Knocker walked the love of his life home, and no doubt would have a bit of the other on the way. Tommy and I walked down Broad Street' had a coffee at an all night café and toddled of home.

CHAPTER 6

A Clap Of A Day

When I awoke the following morning I felt as rough as a bear's arse! and my mattress was wet and sticky. Straight away, I put it down to a wet dream or something like that, until I saw the fluid running out of my penis, and the penny dropped. Ann's daughter, Mary had given me the fucking clap and that was probably the reason I had felt a bit rough for the past couple of days or more. Jesus, what a thing to wake up to!

While I was sat having a cup of tea and a cigarette, I began to have visions of my dick rotting and dropping off, or forever more having a scabby one, knowing that if I did, I was finished as far as having the leg-over was concerned. If I could have gotten hold of Mary, I would have choked the fucking life out of her for what she had done to me!

I had arranged the previous night to meet Tommy around midday, in the Bishopgate pub, and have a couple of beers with him. He was just finishing his first beer when I arrived' When I told him what had happened to me, he roared with laughter and shouted to two or three old fellows who were always in the pub, bright and early, 'George, did you hear that? Riley's got the fucking Clap!'

Needless to say, they all roared their heads off, including the barman.

What a bloody state of affairs I had gotten myself into, even more so now that I had confided in my mate Tommy. It would be all over the fucking area in the next couple of hours, and the strange thing was' that while walking up to meet him I was in two minds whether to tell him or not, just in case he started mouthing off when he was pissed. Once again I had been a right dick!

When they had finished laughing, Tommy agreed to go with me to the General Hospital on Steel house Lane, but said there was no way that he was going in with me' as people might think' he had it as well!

There was a special entrance at the hospital for this kind of disease, and anybody seen going in was automatically tarred with the same brush. We agreed that while I was in there, Tommy would have a drink across the road and wait for me.

Just think for a minute how you would have felt if you had been in my shoes on that day, many years ago!

For the previous three or four months, most of the newspapers and wireless had been warning the public about the effects of venereal disease, and of the epidemic that was taking hold, and that thousands of people all over the world were dying of syphilis. What a thought to have in your mind as you walked into a hospital to show someone your dick, and then having to wait for an hour for the verdict. I wouldn't wish it on my worst enemy, although I could possibly make an exception where my stepbrother was concerned.

When we arrived in the vicinity of the hospital I was relieved to find that the entrance to the section that I wanted was out of the way, down a side street, and well away from the view of the general public. On entering the clinic, I found that there were only two other people waiting.

While sat awaiting my turn, all kinds of things were running through my mind, especially the one concerning the treatment for syphilis in which they have to stick a long needle down the pee-hole in your dick, and when it is fully inserted, they open the needle up similar to an umbrella, and slowly drag it out ripping the scabs off on its way out, and in doing so clearing your pee-hole channel.

Just try to imagine for a moment how you would feel in a situation like this, knowing shortly that you would be in the doctor's surgery, and he would be holding a long thin needle ready to push it down your pee-hole and rip the scabs out. I don't know about you, but putting it mildly I was shitting myself!

What a relief it was on entering the doctor's office to find him sat at his desk in a very relaxed manner. He started to ask questions surrounding the circumstances that had brought me to his surgery. And did I know the name and address off the man or woman that I had caught it from, so that he could send them a letter to come in for a

check-up? When I told him I didn't, he gave me a right bollocking for not wearing protection, and if I ever came to see him again with a similar complaint I would be in big trouble!
He then proceeded to fix a needle and I nearly fainted, even more so when he told me to drop my trousers, but lo and behold, the Lord above must have been smiling down on me that day – I might say for a change - and he stuck it in my arse' gave me some tablets, said I couldn't drink for a week, couldn't have sex, and to come back in a week's time for my final injection, and last but not least sent me on my "now" merry way.

When I was once again out in the fresh air, I felt like a million dollars. After all is said and done, an hour earlier I had thought my sex life was finished, and now here I was on my way to meet my mate in the pub up the road, feeling once again as fit as a fiddle.

However, the feeling didn't last long. The moment I entered the pub, I realized what not having a beer for ten days was going to do to me. What in God's name was I going to do with myself for that length of time?

There was one thing for definite, and that I was totally sure of, after coming out of that clinic – that no matter how many beautiful female bums I managed to get my hands on in the future, I would make quite sure that I never again entered one.

Thinking back on the incident a couple of years later I had to smile to myself for the way my mind had worked on that particular day, as I suddenly realized that a great deal of my trauma at the time was caused by the influence of the media on me and the majority of the British public, even more so on the working classes and their lack of education. They quite enjoyed creating hysteria amongst us, and unfortunately they still do!

I somehow managed for the next four or five days to stay off the beer, and replace it with lemonade, but alas by the following Saturday night my defences broke down, and I was once again one of the lads down at the Railway Club, chatting up the girls and drinking beer.

On the following Monday I called into my works office and presented my boss with a sick note for the following week and needless to say, on hearing what had happened to me, he – just like the others before him burst out laughing, and told me to report to the yard the following Monday.

Oxford

On the following Saturday morning I had my second jab, and was told in no uncertain way never to come back, so it was back to normal at the club, and the young lady I sometimes took home, that was only possible of course if her boyfriend wasn't in attendance, of which I am glad to say he wasn't. After a dance and a few drinks she asked me to take her to her favourite courting spot that I had originally introduced her to, Canal Street.

After the normal preliminaries, I slipped a Durex on before entering her, using the excuse that I didn't want to put her in the family way. Thank God! Once again, my sex life was back in full swing.

Monday morning I reported to the yard where the boss gave me a one-way ticket to a site in Oxford along with an improver's card, and a union card, that in those days you had to produce in order to get on the site, which was totally union-run.

When I arrived I was surprised at the size of the place, it was the main car factory in Oxford where they employed thousands of workers. The firm I was working for was replacing many of its large Boilers and Pipework which had become redundant with age.

There must have been in the region of fifty workers from our company involved in the reformation of the Heating and Ventilating systems so I was hoping that I might just know someone amongst them. By the way, the company I worked for went by the name of Brightside' and in those days they had large sections of the company based in Manchester, Liverpool, and Birmingham' with the only problem they had worker-wise' being the Liverpool section who would down tools for the slightest reason, and at that particular time in the UK they were famous for it. It was the Scargill Era.

When I reported to the site foreman, he sent me down to what I can only describe as a large aeroplane hangar which was being used as a fabrication shop for the new pipe work, which invariably after being set up would be arc welded, and then erected a section at a time.

It didn't take me long to find the charge hand I was looking for who turned out to be a little Irishman called Mick Fahy' who had apparently fixed me up with digs where he and a few of the lads were already staying' which was great news.

He was a little man, five foot and a fart or there abouts, had no upper teeth, had bowed legs, and as I was to find out later a great sense of humour' which made it a joy to work there! In fact, I would go so far as to say it was the best job I had worked on up to that time in my young life.

The following morning I was introduced by Mick to some of my co-workers and assigned to setting up the expansion loops in the large pipe runs of which there were a hell of a lot, but I knew that if I did a good job I would be there for the next few months, and just as important' the money was good, even more so now that I had my improver's card!

The system we were working on was steam, and because of the speed that the steam moved through the large diameter pipe work, every so many yards we had to fit what they called expansion loops to slow down the pressure off it' as it travelled through the large pipe runs' so as to make it more controllable when reaching its destination, i.e. Machine presses etc.

The expansion loops themselves were always U-shaped with right-angled bends ready to be welded to the pipe runs that would follow. It was my job to always be in front of the pipe slingers so as to keep the flow of work on the pipeline from stopping.

For the first couple of weeks I was completely knackered, so after an evening meal and a couple of beers, it was off to my bed so I would be fit for the next day's hard work. In those days, if you worked out of town it would normally be taken for granted that you would work seven days a week with the usual free train ticket every four weeks.

By the time my weekend came up, I was as fit as a fiddle and raring to go. Bear in mind for nearly four weeks I had been making up and slinging large pipe work, consisting of 20-foot lengths with a diameter of 12 inches, twenty foot in the air.

On Home Soil

I arrived back in Birmingham around four o'clock in the afternoon. It was a lovely, warm summer's day with the shoppers out in their droves, no doubt spending their hard earned money on skimpy summer clothes, the Women that is!

The atmosphere was fantastic, I can almost feel it now forty years later and it was a great feeling to be young, even more so with a wad of banknotes burning a hole in my pocket.

I decided to treat myself to some new summer gear along with a new pair of beetle crushers. No doubt some of you old Buggers out there will remember those' from your Teddy boy days.

After an hour of shopping, and rather than catch a bus' I decided on the spur of the moment to walk up Broad Street' which in a roundabout way, led to where I had my bedsit, and on my way I decided to call in the Crown which was about halfway home.

The Crown is still to this day open for business unlike the rest of the pubs on Broad Street that were knocked down in the name of redevelopment and a better way of living' what a load of fucking cobblers! I would go so far as to say that there is more life in the local Cemetery nowadays.

One On It's Own

On entering the Crown, you got the feeling that it had been there forever. The first thing you saw was a massive chandelier hanging from a very high ceiling, which had an original beautifully molded classic style finish. The chandelier itself hung to about ten feet from the floor.

The top half of the walls were covered with old worldly flock paper "which I haven't seen the likes of since" and descended to the height of the chandelier, with the remainder of the walls being finished with a highly polished oak panelling which itself finished at the same height as the fitted seating. To finish the scene off, it had a long polished oak bar, and the floor was likewise' and added to these characteristics was the scattering of some old fashioned Spittoons. That at the very least' would take you back to the late 1880s.

It was the kind of pub that attracted all kinds of Characters. They were, in those days, what the rest of us referred to as Townies, there were Bowler Hats, Cravats, Cigars and Waist coats along with gold watches dangling from chains in the pockets.

The majority of the Crown's clientele ran some kind of business, legal and illegal. There were Bookies and their runners, Nightclub Owners and their minders, well known Scrap Dealers, and many Self-Employed people such as Decorators, Plumbers, Electricians, Steel Erectors and the likes' which all combined' created a very colourful scene and even more so when you allowed for the cigar smoke in the atmosphere.

While I was sitting having my first pint of the day, I spotted a distant relative of mine standing at the far end of the bar drinking whisky as he always did. His name was Jimmy Murphy and he was married to my snotty half sister Eva who I hadn't seen for a good many years, thank God!

Jimmy was definitely a real-life character in every sense of the word. At that moment in time, I would put his age to be his early 40s. He was quite a short man with, what I can only describe, as a ruddy complexion, due no doubt to the vast amounts of whisky he consumed. He was also a bit on the stout side with a bit of a pot belly. Jimmy always wore expensive suits, and anyone looking at him, would not imagine for a moment that this same man had worked for the same company for the past twenty years' on a permanent nightshift. Jimmy, I believe was the night foreman on the maintenance section which in those days was the same as being the top dog. The company he worked for was one of, if not the biggest manufacturers in the world at that time. It was called Lucas and employed thousands of people locally.

He was the type of person who, for a price of course, could supply you with anything you desired' from 'over the wall' as they called it in those days, as in stolen, misappropriated etc. On top of that, he was a bit of a comedian and always good company to be in.

Jimmy saw me at the same time that I saw him. It was very rare that he would shout across a bar room to anyone he wanted to speak to, he would normally catch their attention, nod his head towards the bar and at the same time would point left or right with his hands telling you which side he was inviting you to stand on.

It was only in later years that I realized why Jimmy didn't shout across bars to anyone. It was probably because over the years he had spent so much of his spare time with criminals and the like, in his sideline Business's, that he went out of his way to avoid drawing any attention to himself. After all the stock he came from was Scots and Irish, what a bloody mixture!

Never the less as the Irish would say, He was a fine figure of a man! I decided to have another beer and bought Jimmy a double whisky, much to his delight. After all if I had only bought him a single, there wouldn't have been enough for his throat to notice.

He then started to tell me about his young son, Harry who had just turned sixteen, and had recently put some young girl in the pudding club, and even worse! Had decided to marry her. Even though he had done his best to dissuade him from doing so.

The wedding it seemed was for two weeks time, and was across the road from the Crown at the Birmingham Registry Office, and of course my brothers and I were invited.

By the time I left Jimmy it was later than I had expected and would have taken far too long to get to my bed-sit for a wash and change, so I decided to call at Melia's and have one there' and pick up my gear the next day. I must have knocked on her door for ten minutes without getting any answer, which was very unusual, as her door was always open. I was just about to give up when the woman from next door appeared and informed me that she was over the road in the Bishopgate pub' and that Tom, her Husband had passed away' she also informed me that the funeral had taken place that very morning.

When I entered the bar, Melia was sitting with Harry and a couple of other people that I had seen around. She looked to be in pretty good humour, no doubt helped by a few whiskies and Harry's company. You could always rely on him to lift you out of a depression of any kind. If he was around nowadays he would make a fortune putting people's heads right; come to think of it he could start with mine!

I think, on reflection, she was relieved that Tom had gone' and although I had known that he hadn't been well for more than two years, his death had never the less come as a surprise to me, but according to Harry, Tom had ended up at the point where he could barely breath, so in some ways it had been a godsend.

However, as always, life must go on, so I paid my condolences, got a key from Melia, bought them a round of drinks, slipped her a few quid to help her along' after all, she had always looked after me, even when she was skint and told her I would see her the next day.

By the time I had washed and changed it was around nine o'clock, and I knew that if I wanted to catch Tommy and Knocker I would have to make a beeline for the Albion.

As it turned out, they were just drinking up when I arrived, but on seeing our Hughie was there with his mates I told Tommy and Knocker to carry on without me as I wanted a chat with my brother about old Tom, and would see them later at the Railway Club.

While having a beer I told our Hughie about Tom passing away. Needless to say he was a bit sick about it, but I think it was mostly for melia's sake.

Knocked Up!

A little later, when I got to the Railway Club, Tommy, Knocker, and the love of his life were standing at the bar knocking them back.

After having a chat and a couple of beers, Knocker gave me a nudge and a nod towards the toilets, which was fine by me as I had been bursting for the last ten minutes because some dickhead had started talking to me and I was having a hard time getting away from him. You come across one every now and then!

Where Knocker was concerned, it was bad news he thought he might have knocked his girlfriend up, with her having missed her monthlies, and he had agreed to marry her if she ended up the spout! What do you say in a situation like that? Especially when you know that Knocker thinks the world of her. Ah well, they say love is life, or is it knackered for life? So I wished him and his girl good luck and bought them the best drink in the house, whatever that was at the time.

A Blast From The Past

On Sunday morning following the bad news from knocker! Tommy and I were having a drink in the Bulls Head, and while I was glancing through the open hatch to the lounge to see who was knocking about' I spotted a girl's face that looked familiar to me.

I asked Tommy to take a look to see if he recognized her' He did' and when he mentioned her name, so did I, it was Sally Stern, so I had another glance and noticed that she was sitting with an older woman who looked to be her mother.

It must have been more than twelve months since I had last had a chat with Sally, and I do believe at the time that she was trying to chat me up into giving her one, and I am sorry to say I had better things to do at that moment in time' and gave it a miss.

Sally had obviously seen us looking through the hatch and had recognized me. Half an hour later after the woman we believed to be her mother had left, she came round to the bar to say hello' in a very friendly way I might add.
We talked about things that had happened in the area over the past couple of years, and how she used to fancy me while I was courting one of her friends. That friend by the way was none other than Mary the love of my life.

After another couple of drinks she started to relax and ask me personal things like whether I was courting, where I was working, where I was living etc. She also mentioned that the love of my life had just had her second baby, another boy, and her husband Mike had turned out to be a bit of a tosser.

Apparently Mary's husband hadn't worked for a couple of years or more, and on one or two occasions had knocked her about, not badly but knocked about never the less. It was after one of those instances that her father Harry and her two brothers, who were fifteen and sixteen by that time, waited outside the pub that he used, each armed with the leg of an old chair, and when he came out they beat ten kinds of Shit out of him. However, I do think from knowing Mike in the past, and the way he could handle himself, they had either been very lucky, or he was well and truly pissed when they gave it to him, but whichever it was, it seemed to straighten him out for the better.

By throwing-out time, my mate Tommy was well pissed, and had no doubt worked out what was going down between me and Sally' and wandered off home for his dinner.

After my mates departure I invited Sally for a coffee at an espresso bar which was just around the corner on Broad Street, and for once I hadn't had a lot to drink, which was due in part from all the talking we had done.

By the time we reached the coffee bar we were holding hands, and I already had half a lob on just thinking about it. While drinking our coffee I tried to work out where I could take her that would be private enough.

My bed-sit was the obvious place, but there could be a possible problem with my mate Johnny. Usually, but not always, he would go for a couple of beers with his old man and afterwards his step mother would cook him his Sunday dinner, but it was never guaranteed.

Of course there was always Canal Street but I thought it could be a bit of a problem during the day, as it was also used as a short cut for young couples who wanted to go for a Sunday afternoon stroll along the canal.

After talking it over with Sally she told me in no uncertain way' that there was no way she was going to Canal Street, and gave me an ultimatum' it was to be a bed or nothing!

It turned out to be my lucky day, Johnny was nowhere in sight so I knew I was safe until seven o'clock.

I would now like to take a moment or two to enlighten you on the looks and style of the young lady I would shortly be mounting in my quest for satisfaction. She was quite small, four foot eleven inches to be precise, and that was in her high heels. She was eighteen years of age with short natural blonde hair, plain looking to the point that you would never notice her in a crowd. She was one of those that when she smiled she showed quite a lot off her gums, and to top it off, one of her front teeth was crooked. But that, my friends, is where her let-downs ended. Her body was gorgeous, her breasts were far larger than most girls of her size, her rear end would make your mouth – and possibly other parts of you – water' and that description that I have just given' was that of her wearing clothes; the only way I can describe her without them 'was a small bundle of dynamite'.

I don't know if you can remember so long ago, but in those days it was the norm to find large breasts on mostly tall women, so it was certainly a treat to find this nice large pair on Sally

She wasted no time; the minute my trousers were around my ankles –with my penis as hard as a frozen

Banana, but a bit thicker if you know what I mean – and without any suggestion from me, her lips, along with her crooked front tooth, were sucking my knob-end, and you can rest assured of one thing, until that happens to you on a Sunday afternoon, after a few beers, you haven't been in heaven!

But alas I am one of those people' that before doing anything else' must conquer that hopefully' small hole between their legs, and know if only for that moment in time' that I own them body and soul!

CHAPTER 7

Many years later, while having a beer with my brother Sean, we started reminiscing about some of the characters from our past, and Sally's name popped up. Apparently some months earlier our kid had bumped into her with three or four kids, in the City centre market. The children looked well-nourished and happy little things. And according to him he ended up buying her a cup of tea, and the kids some pop. All I can say to that' is he must have been in a good mood that particular day, as at most times you have a job to get him to pay for his round, if you know what I mean!

They started to talk about people and friends that they both knew, and what had happened to them' invariably the conversation turned to Sally and her family who it seemed, were all happy and doing well.

It was as their conversation progressed that it came out that when she was 13, and extremely mature for her age (a nice size pair of tits at that time) she looked at her mother, who at that time would probably have been in her early 30s, but looked in her forties, and was of a short, stocky build' and suddenly realized that by 30 she would probably be of the same stature as her mother, and with that sudden realization decided there and then that she would fuck as many men as she could get before she got to her mother's stature, and within a few days of that decision had lost her virginity to one of her school friend's fathers' who she told our kid had continued to have sex with her on and off for the next two or three years' In between of which she had sex with any fellow she fancied whether he was married or not, and had only stopped counting when she got to a hundred.

She was only 22 at the time she was having this conversation with our kid. Just think about it logically, what fellow is going to say no to a young girl with a lovely pair of tits and a tight little arse, with her only letdown being her crooked front teeth. You also have to bear in mind that in those days the motto for sex where men were concerned was, 'You don't look at the mantelpiece while you're poking the fire'. I couldn't have put it better myself!

Our conversation then moved to one of our old pals, Mickey from St. Mary Street who used to let me watch him goosing the girls in the little warehouse that he looked after.

Apparently he had taken up with a hard case family called the McDonalds, of which – if I remember rightly– there were four brothers and one sister. His main mate out of them was called Johnny who always had a chat with me whenever we bumped into one another, which was usually in a pub, so I can safely say that we were sort of friendly and got on quite well in one another's company.

According to our kid, about two years after we lost touch with him, mainly due to us moving to Castle

Bromwich, he and Johnny McDonald were in a gang that attacked the Aston mob, which at that time was purported to be the hardest gang in Birmingham. Supposedly the reason for the attack was because on one or two occasions they had been taunting the Ladywood Mob for a showdown.

I remember it well, as it was plastered all over the front page off the Birmingham Mail. According to the report in the paper it was a vicious fight, which included the use of such items of violence as, bicycle chains, razors, knives, knuckle dusters, iron bars etc. Needless to say a lot of the lads who were involved in the fight ended up in prison for a minimum of three months and a maximum of twelve, Johnny and Mickey received six' for their part in the brawl, and according to our kid, when he was released, Mickey settled down and married a lovely looking girl ten years younger than himself, and his wife up to then had borne him two kids, but in my mind knowing Mickey as I did, I had my doubts as to the time it would last.

Back To Oxford

Back to the job in Oxford, which was nearing its end. The boss picked me and another lad to stay until the last to sort out any problems that might arise. The other lad's name was Jimmy; he was a friendly sort of guy. In fact, I sometimes had the niggling feeling that he was over-friendly, but I suppose we all get those feelings at some time or another in our experiences of life.

Jimmy and I worked together for five or six weeks, and most nights we would go to a nearby public house and finish the day off with a game of darts and a few beers. One particular night, while we were having a quiet drink, he started to talk about the Irish he knew from the Birmingham town centre pubs and clubs and it turned out that he knew my stepbrother. To me, hearing his name at that particular time in my life was like showing a red flag to a bull, and I automatically ended up giving my stepbrother a real good slagging, including what I would like to do to him given the opportunity.

It was shortly after my outburst that the job was completed, and I had to report to the yard on the following Monday morning to be assigned to my next job, which I was made to believe from my Boss, would be at Croydon B. Power Station down south, which to me was great news, as I had always wanted to work down that way, and to make things even better the Firm was putting me on a full card.

It was a good feeling to know that they thought enough of me to make me up, I was now a fully fledged Pipe Fitter, and I had no doubt that when it got around to the rest of the firms employees, there would be a lot of back biting from those who had been there much longer than me, and as I found out later, that included my friendly new workmate Jimmy.

A Weekend Leave

Back in Birmingham for the weekend was as good as it always was. In fact, I ended up with Pam again, which was great for me.

By the way I might mention that Oxford was the only place I had worked that I never succeeded in getting my leg over, which was something I was really sick about, so I once again thanked providence for my part time sweet heart Pam!

On the Saturday night there was a crowd of us in one of our local pubs, and on my return from the toilet I heard a bit of a commotion. On entering the bar, lo and behold, there was my stepbrother with a crowd of big swarthy Irishmen baying for blood – mine!

I found out later that my new over-friendly mate Jimmy on his return to Brum, had gone straight to the town centre pub, the Windsor, which at that time was my stepbrother's local, and commenced to tell him about the slagging I had given him, and what I would like to do to him given the opportunity!

So in essence my stepbrother had turned up team-handed to give me the opportunity I desired, and told my mates that if any of them were to interfere, his pals would sort them out. The words were no sooner out of his mouth, when a small dark shadow from the back of our crowd flew over the tops of our heads – in fact one of his hands landed on my shoulder, obviously to give him more momentum – and butted big bully boy Kelly in the mouth.

I heard a little later that it had cost him a lot of money to get his front teeth put right!

That, by the way, was the best news I had heard in years, but back to the fight, the big muscle-bound paddies, some of them with paunches, lasted about three minutes. There were that many of the old-type, solid three-legged stools put over their heads that night, that they were probably frightened to sit on one for the following three weeks, in case it bit them on the arse.

There is no doubt in my mind, on arriving back at their local, that most of them with their heads split open and plenty of blood on them, most of it being their own, would tell their mates that they gave us a right good kicking, just to save face.

After they had made a hasty retreat down the road with us shouting abuse after them, we settled down to a good night's drinking, but only after making a toast to little Johnny Todd for getting the ball rolling with the first nut of the night.

Croydon

I arrived at the job late on Monday afternoon and found that it was only a substation re-pipe, so wasn't surprised to find that I was running the job, with the help of a pipe fitter's mate, a young Irish lad about the same age as myself. I will call him Mick for now.

After sorting out some digs, we went for a wander around the pubs in the town centre to find out where things were going on at the weekend. In one of the pubs we got into a conversation with a Liverpool lad, who had recently moved there after marrying a local girl, and by the end of the night we knew where the best night life was to be found. The job that we were working on was a rush one' where we were expected to work the full seven-day week, but I decided, with my mate's agreement, to work extra hours Monday to Friday, and a half day on the Saturday, which would give us a decent bit of time at the weekends to go gallivanting.

The night life in the town centre, along with the atmosphere, was way out' and the people far more friendly than I had been led to believe by the Liverpool lad we had spoken to on our first night in town. In retrospect I think the Scouser was probably getting a bit of the backlash for the fact that the Scousers weren't very well liked, mainly because of their militancy, which was forever in the newspapers. Where on the other hand' where the Brummies were concerned they had no such problem, which was probably because Marlene was all the rage at the time.

We wandered around two or three bars, seeing if we could pull a couple of the local girls and after a couple of hours we were just about to give up when we decided to finish our night off with a couple of drinks in good old Yates's Wine Lodge.

Believe it or not, as we entered Yates's, there at the end of the bar standing on their own, were two smart young ladies drinking white wine. I will take just a minute or two to give you an idea of what my Irish mate was about. Apart from being just short of six foot, he had a wide-open, reddish face with plenty of humour in it, but nevertheless looked to all the world what he was – an Irishman, and an extremely likeable one.

It was Mick's turn to get the beers in, and he didn't hesitate in asking the young ladies if they would like to have a drink, while adding that we had just arrived from Birmingham on a contract job, and didn't know anyone in Croydon' thankfully they accepted

I have no doubt that most of you at sometime in your lives will have heard of the Blarney Stone. Even to this day I believe that Mick had swallowed it. The patter he could come out with' was nobody's business, and in no time at all we were laughing and joking with our new found female friends.

Once again it turned out to be the mother and daughter thing, and I have no doubt you will remember the last mother and daughter I had met and the clap of a time I had had with them. Ah well, here we go again, 'Into the valley of death rode the six hundred!

At closing time, they invited us back to their flat for a cup of coffee. I think it is about time that I gave you some information on the style and looks of these two young ladies. The mother looked to be in her early or middle thirties, and quite tall, with long, silky-brown hair down past her shoulders which probably made her look younger than she really was. She was of a slim build with nice legs, and a nice sized pair of 'Bristol Cities' to go with them.

The daughter, on the other hand, was around five foot two or three, but much more dainty than her Mother. She had small breasts, blonde hair and blue eyes, and although at first sight I had noticed that her mother's legs were nice, her daughter's were even more so. Have you ever noticed that on the odd occasion when you have had a few drinks how the mind can play tricks on you, especially if you have half a lob on at the time? It makes a woman you are chatting up seem more attractive than she really is which invariably the morning after you have given her one or two the night before, makes you look for any excuse, to make a hasty retreat. I am glad to say this wasn't to be one of those times.

Their apartment was very smart as were the clothes they wore. It turned out later that they were both air hostesses but had only been doing it for two or three weeks.

We settled for a coffee, some soft music, and a bit of a smooch to go with it. After a little kissing and rubbing up against one another I was once again like a stick of Blackpool rock. My girl's name was Jenny and her mother was called Maureen, who by this time had disappeared with Mick, you can no doubt guess to where!

With her Mother doing a disappearing act Jenny had unzipped my trousers' and without hesitation had taken my penis in her lovely little hands, giving it a gentle massage while I, on the other hand, had her lovely shaped little tits in my hands, giving the nipples on them a good sucking which was turning her on in no uncertain way. I am starting to get funny feelings just thinking and writing about this.

It wasn't long before we ended up in her bedroom, with both of us stripped bullock naked, and what a luscious little thing she was. I must have kissed every inch of her, including her beautiful rear end. And thank God, for me it was no longer taboo!

We were at it all night, and what that girl did not do to me isn't worth mentioning, and I daren't mention all the things I did to her, in case someone locks me up!

Mick and I ended up staying the night and I was awoken from my lovely dreams at about 10am with a nice cup of tea, a kiss and a lovely smile. What more could a man ask for? It seemed to me that I must have done something right for a change!

After having a wash and getting dressed, I sauntered into the living room, and what a sight met my eyes! Mick was sat there with his arm around Maureen with a smile on his face, staring into her big blue eyes as though mesmerized by them. To any onlooker, it looked as though they were smitten with each other, and there was no doubt in my mind that something serious was going on between them.

After a good breakfast, we invited them out for a Chinese meal later that evening, and a bit of music somewhere else afterwards, which I am happy to say they accepted, this was followed by a big kiss from Jenny, and a lift back to the centre of town where Mick and I nipped into the nearest pub for a couple of liveners which we were in dire need off. After a good afternoon sleep, and a nice shower we were, 'out early doors' as in opening time, so we could have a few pints before meeting the girls.

In one or two of the pubs that we called into, we got into a conversation with a barman or two. Most good barmen are very nosey people, and I have found wherever I have worked' and where my accent was different to that of the locals, the barman always wanted to know what I was doing in his neck of the woods, but at the same time would put you wise to where the girls were, along with the in places to go.

On reflection it seems to me that the only things that interested me – and the great majority of my fellow beings in those days, were wine, women and song. They were the beginning and end-all of life itself. In retrospect, it was a ridiculous way to live, and at the end of the day the only way we could have materialized into that kind of society was because of the total lack of education that was available to the working classes, and for no other reason whatsoever!

***

We met Maureen and Jenny at the Chinese restaurant at nine o'clock, where we found the girls already seated and drinking a glass of wine. Now if that wasn't two women full of confidence I don't know what is.

We all enjoyed the meal including plenty of stories and humour from Mick' and at the end of which, we decided because of a hard day's work the following day we would take the girls home, have a quick leg-over, and get back to the digs for a good night's sleep.

The girls themselves were back on duty the following afternoon, and wouldn't be back until the early hours of the following Saturday morning.

All through Monday at work Mick never let up on talking about Maureen and how fantastic she was, and that he really fancied her in a big way. What was I supposed to say to that? Only that he should wait until he got to know her better before pouring his heart out to her.

It was Wednesday of the same week that our boss in Birmingham phoned me, and asked if we could help him out that weekend on a rush job, one that we referred to in those days as a 'ghoster' at the Tate and Lyle sugar factory in Canning Town.

A ghoster would start on a Friday evening after the workers had left for the weekend, and then you were expected to work non-stop, right through until the Monday morning when the factory reopened for its workers. Up until then I had been on two or three of them for the company, and had always enjoyed the experience, and especially where the money was concerned.

Every hour throughout the weekend was paid at treble time, it was similar to two or three week's wages in a weekend. The only problem with earning that kind of money if you were single' was the large amount of deductions that the taxman would take. The normal criteria for this type of work, where any company was concerned, was that by the Monday morning before Tate and Lyle's hundreds of workers returned to work the contract had to be completed and the factory ready for production. If, for any reason, it wasn't completed on time the company would be in big trouble, and face large fines. It was also recognised by our company's workers that if you didn't go out of your way to help them when these Ghosters came around, you would normally end up regretting it for the rest of your time working for them, which normally wouldn't be much longer if the boss had anything to do with it!

Right up until Friday midday, Mick was all for going to Tate and Lyle's, then out of the blue he decided against it as he had been waiting all week for Saturday to come when he would be able to see Maureen again, obviously her now being the main love of his life.

I argued and argued with him, even using the fact that it was well-known that any workers who stepped out of line, nearly always ended up the road without a job, but "the dick" wouldn't change his mind' and where losing his job was concerned, he wasn't bothered.

By now, it was quite obvious to me that he had got it bad for Maureen, and there was nothing I could do about it, and when he asked me to ring the office to tell them he had sprained his wrist, and wouldn't be fit for the weekend, I did do, but was told by my boss that he wouldn't be able to carry on working on our own job Until I returned from Canning Town. Needless to say, Mick was a bit sick with this news.

Throughout my life it has never failed to amaze me how some fellows do, and probably always will, take the chance of losing a fantastic job, for the face of an attractive woman and the promise of a leg-over, as shown in this case. Isn't love grand?

Overall, it had cost Mick the equivalent of three weeks' money in extra wages or more, and all for the sake of a bloody leg-over, what a dickhead!

When I arrived, late Friday afternoon, at Tate and Lyle I had to report to the canteen where the foreman would sort out our work areas. The canteen was chock-a-block with bodies; there must have been fifty or more of our lads, and God knows how many belonging to other companies, it certainly looked to me at the time that it was going to be one hell of a hectic weekend!

It wasn't long after my arrival that the foreman gathered us together, and told us in no uncertain terms that anyone caught dossing would be up the road, while adding that this particular job was an important one for the company, and if it wasn't finished on time they would lose thousands of pounds by the extra hour. To say it was hard work would be to put it mildly, but nevertheless we had finished it off just before midnight on Sunday.

On Monday when I arrived back on the job in Croydon. It was the early afternoon and I was glad to see that my mate had been going at it great guns.

Before I could get a word in edge ways he started to talk about the girl' but I wasn't in the mood for it and told him it would keep until we had finished for the day.

It was after 7pm when we finished having once again got plenty of work done.

On our way back to the Digs We called at our usual Café' had something to eat and Mick began to tell me what had happened in my absence' OH! What a fucking Dickhead!

I just could not believe it. All I can say in his defence' is' at that particular time he must have been walking around with his Cock up his Arse' and had forgotten that at the time we had been first told about the weekend at Tate's we had stuck a note in the girls letter box telling them what had happened' and we would get in touch with them on our return.

Of course, being an Irishman and a very nice fellow, he was nevertheless as thick as two short planks, and hadn't thought to put a second note through telling them that there was a change of plan. (no disrespect to the Irish' I love em!)

But I must say at this juncture, that he did at least manage to remember that the girls wouldn't return home until the early hours of Saturday morning, and would probably be asleep for most of the day, Because of this he decided to call on them at seven o'clock in the evening.

From all accounts I believe Maureen had a bit of a shock on opening her front door and coming face-to-face with the love of her life, well for the previous weekend at least. Mick, being the impetuous type of chap that he was, immediately picked her up bodily' and without further ado stuck a big pair of lips' on hers!

I think in retrospect, and so does Mick, that had he not taken this action the next fifteen minutes that followed would never have been!

Mick with his lips still glued to her mouth' and having now reached the living room' Maureen by this time doing her utmost to get free from his strong arms and crushing lips' and with not a word having passed between them since seeing each other again' not even to say hello! As he carried her into the lounge, Lo and behold, there sat on Mick's love seat, where he had last given her one, bent over the back of it, I might add! Were two smart looking young fellows, dressed up like Dogs dinners, and ready for the road. Mick obviously thought they were ready for the root!

According to him, on seeing these smart young Chaps sitting there' waiting for the girls to get ready, he completely lost it! and started slagging Maureen, for amongst other things being an old cow and a slag, and if that wasn't enough, and with him still holding her in his arms with her feet off the ground commenced to throw her on top of the two fellows sitting on their love seat.

At this action the bigger fellow out of the two was up and swinging at Mick calling him all the fancy names people called the paddies in those days, and a few more besides. Without further ado, Mick butted him, and he went to sleep on top of his mate, while Maureen in the meantime was still struggling to get off Mick's love seat where he had thrown her.

After telling Maureen to stay out of Yates's wine lodge while he was still in town or he would break her fucking neck, he left them to it, shouting to the fellows on his way out that he hoped they both ended up with a dose of the clap.

At work, and anywhere else we went that week, I couldn't help laughing when I thought of it, and even to this day thinking back to it, it brings a smile to my face. That would have to be the shortest true love story of all time. You can rest assured of one thing, it cost Mick a lot of extra rounds in the pub, to compensate me for the loss of my little love, Jenny and the wee hole between her legs. After all is said and done I only wanted to borrow mine.

CHAPTER EIGHT

The Café

We had two weeks left on the job, and ever since starting it, we had used the same café for all our meals, and would invariably chat up the waitress and have a laugh with her. From what we could gather, she was married to a nice fellow, and had a two-year-old son by him, but sometimes she still got bored with her life, and so to alleviate this she would have a night out once a week. She even went so far as to mention the name of the pub, including where it was situated.

Apparently her husband looked after the baby on Friday nights when she went out with some of her friends, and alternatively she had him on Saturday night so her husband could do likewise with his mates.

We both decided to call at this pub on the last-but-one Friday night before we finished the job. It was more so for the craic than anything else, and at the same time we could buy our friendly waitress a going away drink.

Mick by this time, was a reformed character where falling in love was concerned. He had learned the hard way, and had decided from there on in' he would spend the next two or three years Podging anything that was going, before settling down with a love of his life. To my mind as far as this statement from Mick was concerned, seeing would be believing.

As was normal we were out early doors on Friday Evening' and after a couple of drinks in Yates's decided as previously agreed to find the Pub that our Waitress used' on the of chance that we would like it' and if we didn't it would give us ample time to find somewhere better.

As it happened, we were quite surprised at the size of the place, and its smart furnishings. Added to that' it was a quarter full, which we found a bit unusual that early in the evening.

By the time we had downed a couple of beers, the live music came on, and ten minutes later the women started pouring through the front doors, half of them had obviously had a few drinks, and were singing and shouting at the top of their voices. By the time we had finished our third drink the place was practically heaving, with a large percentage of the clientele being lovely young ladies out for a night on the town.

As usual, Mick didn't waste any time getting into conversation with a crowd of young good looking girls, who looked to be enjoying his jokes, and I can still hear them now. The Englishman, the Irishman and the Scotsman! That was how all of his jokes began, and in reality you would have to be half pissed to laugh at them. God bless him. It was the way he told them!

Suddenly, out of nowhere, our waitress appeared with a few of her mates. She looked like a different girl than the one we knew' She was a little beauty and nothing whatsoever like the young girl who had served us for the past two or three weeks, and it didn't take me long to tell her so.

It seemed, after talking with her for a little while, that there was a verbal agreement between everyone who was employed by the café, that they must play down their looks to a 'Plain Jane' stereotype – as in plain and ordinary' so as not to have the customers spending their time ogling and tapping them up instead of eating their food, thus ensuring a larger turnover off seats, and of course a bigger profit for the boss. He, incidentally, saw them right with a few extra quid in their wages at the end of the week. It sounded good business to me, and it was certainly the first time I had ever heard of a lovely looking young woman being paid extra to make herself look dowdy.

By this time Mick was back in our company, and chatting with some of our waitress's friends, and I did notice that a couple of them looked very interested in him.

Up to that moment, we didn't even know her name, probably because we always referred to the girls who worked there as 'Luv', 'Darling' or 'Sweetheart'. As it happened her name was Jane, and don't think for one moment that I am going to come out with that old cliché, 'Me Tarzan, You Jane', even though after giving her a good coat of looking at, I did feel a bit like him in my trousers. At the same time as I was feeling this way Mick as usual had got into his stride with one of Jane's mates whom he now had out on the dance floor, so Jane and I joined them.

At throwing-out time, the girls invited us to their regular Friday night nightclub, which came as a bit of a surprise to us, but apparently her agreement with her husband on a Friday night included that she could stay out with her friends until the club closed at three o'clock in the morning! Mick, was certainly breaking the barriers down between him and his young lady, to the point that he was now kissing her while his large hands were busy fondling her lovely little arse. At seeing this I started in on Jane with a good response, in fact far better than I had ever expected. Which wise man once said, 'Still waters run deep'? After groping one another for ten minutes while waiting for a taxi, I suddenly realized that the young lady in my arms was like a full dam ready to burst her banks.

When the taxi arrived, Mick's girl invited us to her house which was apparently only a short distance from the club, for a couple of drinks before we went there, as it didn't liven up for another hour or more.

On arrival at the house, which was a semi-detached, smart inside and out, we settled down to a spot of music and a bottle of beer, it must have been less than fifteen minutes after entering the house that Mick disappeared with his girl.

It wasn't to be long after Mick vanished that Jane and I headed for her friend's spare bedroom, with Jane leading the way, holding my now rock-hard penis in her hand. Her dam had burst, and Jesus, what a little raver she had become! I must have podged her for two hours or more, non-stop, and this time, for the first time in a long time, zeroed in on her rear end where up until then only her husband had tread!

I think her husband must have tread very carefully where her lovely little arse was concerned, as I found it to be as tight as a Virgins, and thoroughly enjoyed making her squeal as I rammed it home, balls and all. And that young lady loved every minute of it.

When we were finished with our lust, I had a quick beer while Jane smartened herself up ready for home and her husband.

While in the taxi she told me it was the best sex she had had since being married, and the fact that her husband was always tired had probably added to her enthusiasm and enjoyment. She asked me around to her house around midday on the following Wednesday for another session, it being her day off from the café. I didn't need any coaxing, and said I would be there with my boots blacked.

Mick was over the moon with his new girlfriend, who was divorced, and had told him that she had fallen for him in a big way the moment she had set eyes on him, enough so, as to try to get him to pack his job in, move in with her' and take up employment locally. Good on you, Mick!

The following night, which was a Saturday, I had a quick couple of drinks with Mick before he set off for his date, but not without me warning him about this 'real love' thing.

Can you just imagine, me, five foot and a fart telling a lad the size of Mick, and built like a brick shithouse to behave himself in love? In fact, if I remember correctly, his answer went something like, 'Get stuffed you fucking Arsehole. See you later.' It was to be Sunday afternoon before I was to see Mick again, and he was certainly worse for wear.

As always whenever I had no particular place to go, I invariably ended up in Yates's, where I am glad to say there was always a bit of something going on.

Ten minutes after entering, I got into a conversation with a couple of Scots lads I had been chatting to the previous weekend, when one of them informed me that Jenny had been in a couple of times asking if anyone had seen me knocking about, I decided even as good as she had been, she couldn't be up the spout after a week.

I was on my second or third Beer when yours truly appeared at my side, and planted an affectionate kiss on my cheek, chattering away at the same time about Mick having come around to their flat, and doing what he had done. She then explained to me that what Mick had done at their apartment wasn't important to her, it was the fact that because of it, I hadn't been around to see her. Obviously it seemed to her that because of Mick's action when it wasn't anything to do with her I had stood her up, and that I now owed her an apology for not meeting her when I was supposed to do so on my return from Tate and Lyle. So I gave her one, an apology that is, and another and another but that was a bit later on.

Her mother eventually came up in the conversation. It turned out that she was already engaged and had been for the past couple of years, to a well off Business man, who at the time that her Mother had met Mick was abroad on business. She assured me that her mum had to be very attracted to a man to go to bed with him, and there was no way that she would hop into bed with any Tom, Dick or Harry.

The two fellows that had been at their apartment were her older brother and his best mate, with whom she had gone to school. However, when questioned further on the matter, she did admit that he had been trying to get into her knickers for a long time, but without any success! What are you, Mick? He would obviously cause trouble in an empty house, and not even know it! As it happened, Jenny's mother was staying at her Boyfriend's for the night, so we would have the apartment to ourselves. When we arrived at the apartment Jenny changed into a pair of flimsy, see-through Pyjamas, and to say it was a turn-on would be the understatement of the year. I later found out that she had had them made in India on one of her flights there, out of a specially coated material that when it touched her nipples and love patch it titillated them to the point of arousal. Can you just imagine wearing Pyjamas that had that effect on you? Your cock would probably be standing to attention forever more.

Bristol

On the Tuesday, we received our orders to return to Birmingham on the following Friday, followed by the yard on Monday for new orders. What do you tell the girls? In my case, nothing, but I did see my little waitress on Wednesday afternoon at her place, and had a very pleasant time, and a good finish to the job.

After a quiet weekend, which I badly needed, I turned up at the yard on the Monday morning for my new orders.

It was to be Bristol, and my good mate Mick was going with me, so if nothing else the craic would be good. When we arrived on site, the job consisted of piping separate central heating systems into three blocks of newly-built, high-rise flats complete with radiators, so it certainly looked as though we would be there for quite a while.

I did find it a bit strange at the time to be installing central heating in steel pipe, when the norm was copper.

I found out later, after talking to the site foreman, that the powers-that-be had decided on this course of action after over spending on the overall construction. Copper at that time was extremely expensive compared to steel pipe, and unlike copper, steel could be installed far quicker and at a third of the cost, which to all intents and purposes sounded fantastic. It was just a pity that some of the whizz kids didn't bother to look a few years down the road to the time that it would rust, and become obsolete.

We started work on the rising mains the following morning, and were getting well into it, when I heard a familiar voice calling my name. When I turned my head to see who it was, I couldn't believe my eyes. It was old Acker and Jimmy Jones, who I hadn't seen in months.

Now, my friends, you had better believe me when I say that two of the biggest head cases from central

Birmingham had just arrived in our midst. Jimmy lived two doors down the road from one of my best mates, Micky Smith, and had come over from Ireland at about the same time that I had, but still had a tiny bit of an Irish accent while I had none. Jimmy was well- built, with rugged good looks and a great sense of humour. The women couldn't get at him for falling over themselves trying' and to top it off, there wasn't a day's work in him. If that wasn't enough for a man 22 years of age, he was just going through his second divorce.

Acker was a wholly different kettle of fish. At that particular time, he was much older than us, probably in his late thirties, and if you had ever had the pleasure to know him you would probably have realised that as a young lad at school he must have been on the clever side. An example of the way Acker was is easily summed up. If anybody who used our locals wanted to know when Queen Victoria was born he had only to ask our Acker, and they would receive the correct answer, and that went for almost any other topic.

From the general hearsay in the area he had lost it in his early 20s, when he was certified as an incurable alcoholic. I do believe there was such a disease in those days, or perhaps we were that thick that we believed everything that people told us! Nevertheless you can take it from me Acker was definitely one. It was also a fact that he was well-known in the area to be the only one to have actually served a six year apprenticeship as a plumber after leaving school at the age of fourteen, and came out of his time' certificate-wise at the age of 21, when it is said he took to the drink in a big way, and had done very little work since.

Needless to say I was amazed to see him on the same site as myself. In fact, I think it may have crossed my mind on seeing him that perhaps he had followed me for the price of a drink. Oh, if only he had!

A couple of days after Acker's arrival, he and Jimmy were working with me and Mick on the fourth floor. It was somewhere around ten o'clock in the morning, when we suddenly heard a woman screaming at the top of her voice, 'Where's that dirty bastard that pissed my bed last night? If I get hold of him I will break his fucking neck!' Yes, you've guessed right, it was Acker she was looking for.
It was only after looking over the balcony, and seeing a 20-stone woman waving a dirty white bed sheet in the wind, and on top of that her seeing us at the same time we saw her, that she started to make her way towards the stairwell entrance, effing and blinding.

She was shouting to anyone who would listen to her, what she was going to do to Acker when she got hold of him, but all of the time Acker was rolling around laughing his head off. He wasn't bothered, what with her weight she wouldn't make it to the first floor!

The outcome, I am sorry to say, was Acker getting the sack, and thrown off the job immediately, and needless to say, all of the lads had to dip into their pockets, to find him his train fare home, and of course a few bob for a bottle of beer.

After the departure of Acker, the foreman decided because of the speed that we were carrying out the work before Acker left that I could keep Jimmy with me as a second mate rather than send him back to the yard.

Once again, our main starting point at the weekend was good old Yates's Wine Lodge in the centre of Bristol where, after a short time, we began to make friends.

One of the lads we mated up with was called Frank who was a few years older than us, and had a lovely looking girlfriend, that we found out at a later date was 17 years of age, and full of it. In fact, in retrospect, he was probably old enough to be her father.

The in-thing at that time was for carry-outs at closing time to different friends' houses or flats with plenty of rock'n'roll music going on. Invariably, the majority were couples, and once the boyfriend was out of it on drink, probably helped along with a few puffs of cannabis, you would always come across one of the girlfriends who wanted to play.

It was at one of these parties that Jimmy met a young girl who was an absolute stunner, and most of the lads would have given their right arm for the chance to get between her legs. He started to go out with her quite a lot so we knew he was quite serious about her, as normally if he wasn't he would dump them.

In the meantime Mick and I carried on going to parties, most weekends, usually with Frank and his girlfriend who we were getting to know quite well by then.

Incidentally, do any of you old buggers out there remember the middle '50s and early '60s, when the majority of girls had lovely legs, and those were the main turn-on for the male species? In fact, I would go so far as to say that they were the first part of a female that you looked at before deciding to tap her up, or not.

Just think about it for a minute or two, it's got to be 99 percent certain, even in this day and age, that if you see a girl walking down the street with a lovely pair of legs, it automatically follows that she will always have a lovely, mouth-watering posterior at the top of them. On the other hand, you rarely see a good- looking woman with attractive legs nowadays, and in fact I would go so far as to say that in my own personal opinion a good 70 to 80 percent of young women, including most of the good-looking ones have horrible legs, and the biggest godsend to the girls of today, are of course trousers. Hence we now have to weigh them up the best we can, by the shape of their arse, and at best that only amounts most times, to pot luck.

Also bear in mind that when you have got a young lady in the right position to give her one, and as most times that this happens, you will automatically have a lob-on at the same time, then you manage to get her pants off her, the last thing you are going to look at are her yampy legs, as the only thing in your mind at this stage of the game is to get your engorged penis into that wet little honey pot between her legs….After that piece of useless information I will get back to our nightlife in Bristol, and some of the parties we went to where most of the ingredients were drink, women, soft drugs and last, but not least, the good old rock'n'roll. It was inevitable that there would be trouble every so often, which was mainly caused by women and their lack of inhibitions once under the influence of the drink and drugs.

Just imagine for a moment a living room and kitchen full to overflowing of young drunken men and women, with some of the young girls going out of their way, on occasion, to press themselves against you while passing by with their drinks, trying in some cases to turn you on, and invariably doing so.

On top of that, you have some of the young lads, 17 or 18 years of age passed out, leaving their young-Girlfriends full of it and raring to go, with Mick and me standing on the sidelines waiting to step in and supply their needs.

We certainly managed to do that on two or three occasions, but sometimes with dire consequences, like the boyfriend walking into the toilet as we were just about to slip one into the love of his life. Or, on the other hand, you would have girls coming on to other girls' boyfriends, and all hell would break loose.

Every now and then, while at some of these parties, I would end up having a dance or two with Frank's girlfriend, whose name was Ellie. Quite often, when she was pissed, she would get what seemed at the time to be a bit over-friendly with me and Mick, but we didn't think too much of it, as we were normally too busy trying it on with some girl or another. Anyway, at the end of the day we decided that she was just trying to lead us up the garden path with nothing at the end of it.

Once again, we were to be wrong in our analysis of Ellie. It happened on a Saturday night at one of the parties where a large percentage of the partygoers were a bit on the young side - 15 or 16 years old – and causing a lot of hassle, as kids of that age always manage to do.

Out of the blue, Frank and Ellie decided they had had enough of these young idiots and decided to go home early for a change and invited us to their pad to have a couple of drinks with them.

We were a bit surprised at their invitation, it being the first time they had invited us to their place in the six weeks or more that we had been knocking about with them. We had only been there for half an hour, sitting comfortably with a glass of beer and having a good laugh, when Ellie suddenly changed the rock'n'roll music for some soft, smoochy stuff, and out of the blue asked in a sexy voice 'Which one of you good-looking lads is going to dance with me? Before either of us could answer, she had pulled Mick up, saying as she did so, 'Come on Mick, show me what you can do!'

They hadn't been dancing for more than twenty seconds when she started pushing her pelvis against Mick's upper thighs, while Mick had his hands resting on her very attractive rear end, slowly fondling her cheeks when he had his back to us.

Perhaps he thought that, in the dimmed lighting, Frank wouldn't notice what he was doing. Nothing could have been further from the truth. Come the end of the record, she turned to me. 'Come on, it's your turn, Charlie.'

It took only a minute for my cock to come to attention with her rubbing her lower half against me. All of a sudden, she put her lips against my ear and whispered, 'I know what you want, you naughty boy. Why don't you ask Frank if you can fuck me in the bum? He loves to see me being sodomised by a younger man, and loves to wank off while they are ramming it into me. In fact, it's one of the few times he gets hard enough to fuck me himself. Go on, ask him! He won't bite you.

It was at that exact moment that Frank shouted above the music, 'Come on, Ellie! Let's get this party going! Show these young lads what it's all about. Go and change into something more sexy and give us all a treat!'

While she was gone, I sat down again and took a sip of my beer, saying to Frank, 'Your missus is a great dancer Frank.' He answered, with a burst of laughter, 'Charlie, my boy, I think you were doing a bit more than just dancing with her, but I have to admit it turned me on a bit watching you and Mick taking turns fondling her tight little Arse.'

It took Ellie quite a while to change. In fact I was beginning to think they were both having us on, but suddenly there she was, in all her glory, with nothing but a pair of silk see-through pantaloons on her lovely body, and without even thinking about it we all gave her a round of applause, which she seemed to lap up.

Frank was the first to speak. ‘Turn around Ellie and slowly pull your pantaloons down over those lovely little arse cheeks. You know it helps me get a lob on luv.’

Swaying to the soft music, she did just that, and what a sight! She had an absolutely beautiful arse, small, round and smooth, and if that wasn’t enough, you could see her vagina hanging down in line with her bum cheeks as she bent over while slipping her pants off. What a delightful sight to behold on a Saturday night around midnight, or any night for that matter, especially if you’re feeling full of it!

‘You know what to do luv’ Frank said, as he stripped off, and my God – what a dick he had on him! I think he must have inherited it from a donkey. After all is said and done, none of us know who our ancestors were. By the size of Mick’s, it was very likely that he had come from a line of Jack Russels. Sorry, mate!

By the time we were all stripped off I couldn’t wait to get at her, but I knew from the tone of Frank’s voice that we would have to follow his directions. Perhaps he had to organize it in a certain way in order to fulfil his fantasy. In the meantime, Ellie had put two large, flat cushions on top of one another, and was now knelt behind them.

I was beginning to wonder what the fuck was going on, when suddenly, out of the blue, Frank lay down on the carpet resting his head on the two cushions.

Once Frank's head was in position, Ellie moved forward with her knees wide open until her vagina was directly over Frank's mouth, leaving him a clear view of the cocks, in their turn ramming into her rectum, while he, Frank had his tongue stuck up her vagina, while wanking himself off at the same time.

Then came the orders, 'Mick, you get your dick in her mouth! Charlie, you up her arse, and I want you to ram it into her, and don't worry about Ellie. She loves a bit of pain, while adding, but the most important thing, is when you're near to pumping it to her, I want you to pull your cock completely out of her arse' and re-insert, just your knob-end and foreskin three or four times before you finish her off, so I can get a full view of the knob itself entering her arse while my tongue is inside her, 'But make sure that you pump your cream into her Arse, and not over my face!'

These last few words from Frank brought a burst of laughter from me and Mick, along with giggles from Ellie, what a bloody turn on! Nobody would believe this in a million years.

As I lined my cock up for getting into her lovely rear end, which was already moving backwards and forwards from the effects of Frank's tongue, I managed to catch her on one of her backward movements, and drove the full length of my Penis into her dry Anus, bringing a scream from her which I have no doubt would have been much louder, but for the fact that Mick's dick was now buried in her throat.

When, on the odd occasion, my mind drifts back to that night I believe I can still feel my knob and foreskin going in and out of her tight little arsehole three or four times before coming for the first time in her rectum, And that really did take Frank over the top. What a raver, she burnt the three of us out; it must have been four o'clock in the morning when we left them, with my foreskin red raw.

Later on that day, Mick and I agreed that the highlight of the evening was seeing Frank's rock-hard donkey's dick going into her inch by inch, with her squirming all over the floor, trying to take all of it.

We were invited for a repeat session the following weekend which turned out even more interesting than the first one, helped by the fact that another couple took part.

We were as sick as chips when we were taken off the job, supposedly over some error or other, concerning the company's contract with its client, but nevertheless the Boss reckoned once the problems had been ironed out, he would send us back to finish the job.

After helping in the clearing of the site, we had to report to the yard in Birmingham where I was a bit sick when they split me and Mick up, sending him down to London, where at the time they were short of pipe fitters mates, and me to a job on a new school under construction in West Bromwich on the outskirts of Birmingham. I am very sorry to say, that was the last time I ever saw Mick. Three weeks later, I left the job because the out-of-town work had dried up.

CHAPTER NINE

Late 60s ?

It was the late '60s and work was a bit on the tight side in the pipefitting trade, even more so where out-of-town work was concerned. It was around this time that my brother Sean was working for a steel erecting company in Birmingham, near the Ivy Bush in Edgbaston. It was, if I remember correctly a very small company of half a dozen or so workers, with two or three of them in the fabrication shop where they made up the steel RSJ's to the right size for piecing together on site.

The main qualities you needed for this kind of work, apart from using nuts and bolts, was a good head for heights' along with the bottle! As we called it in those days, to swing standing centrally on large steel girders as the crane took them of the ground and brought them into position.

One of the lads would be sat on one end of the steel RSJ with another on the other end' and as normally happened, with myself in the middle. It was my job, when we were at the right height, which could sometimes be hundreds of feet of the ground, to use my weight on the two arms of the sling to swing the steel girder into position, so my mates at either end could slip their nuts and bolts into place, and tighten them up. When both ends had been correctly fixed to the existing steelwork, I would then sit down in the centre of the girder so as to allow the crane driver to lower the hook that held the sling' sufficiently, so as to allow me to disconnect it from the hook, and I was then left to shimmy along on my backside to one end, and make my own way down to the ground, or to the height of a ladder if we had one. It could be bloody hard work but the money was always good for that kind of work.

I can remember quite clearly arriving with my new boss, a Mr Peters, who was the sole owner of the company, and a very posh old chap. At that particular time, he must have been knocking on 70 years of age.

It was nine o'clock in the evening when we entered the only hotel in Fort William in Scotland. For the first time in my life I was actually booked into a four star hotel, and before going to bed I could leave my shoes outside my door for cleaning. Now if that ain't the bee's knees, I don't know what is!

I don't know what it is like today but at that time, there were only half a dozen houses in Fort William, hence the only reason for the boss to book us in to the hotel, which we liked a lot, but it wasn't really our cup of tea. On top of that the chance of a leg-over and a good piss-up were non-existent, so it would be all work and no play.

When we left the hotel the next morning, with our shoes polished, we were in for another surprise. To get to the job we had to board a large barge that took us a couple of hundred yards to what I could only assume was the other side of the village, where there was no housing whatsoever.

What a godforsaken place for anyone to go for a bit of work! On thinking back, I wouldn't have wished it on my worst enemy. When we reached the site we found that all the steel and other equipment necessary to get the job finished had already arrived.

After checking the site plans, and weighing up how long it would take us without going at breakneck speed to complete the job, we gave the boss a time of five weeks, which he was well suited with. On top of that we had a verbal agreement with him, that if we decided to work extra hours to get it finished quicker, he would undertake to pay us the balance of the five week price as a bonus, and at the same time would save himself hotel bills. We shook hands on it – that stood for something in those days – and started work there and then.

The job would and, in fact, did become a paper pulp mill, and as far as I know is still one to this day.

Three weeks later the steelwork was finished, thank God! What a fucking godforsaken place to send any man. While we were in Scotland, the boss asked us to stop off and do a small job on our way back to Birmingham and the human race. The place we stopped off at was called Dunfermline, in Fife! another god forsaken place. Even the pubs closed at nine o'clock in the evenings, and but for the help of a local lad who could get us into one or two pubs after time, that place would have been as big a nightmare as Fort William had been.

It was midday on a Monday when we eventually arrived back in Birmingham. I had a word with the boss and with a bit of coaxing he agreed that I could have the rest of the week off to recuperate a little from all the hours I had worked over the past few weeks, knowing full well what kind of recuperation I would be looking for, as in mates, booze and women. He agreed to it, so long as the following Monday I would go to a job up north for a few months, which at the time suited me down to the ground.

Rochdale - Greater Manchester

My new job was based in a small town called Rochdale in Lancashire, at a very large asbestos factory, named Turner Bros. By the way, there was nothing known about the side effects of asbestos in those days.

I decided to travel up to Rochdale late on the Sunday afternoon ready for work the following day. It must have been quite late when I left Brum, as I clearly remember arriving in Rochdale at around 11pm.

This was in the middle of winter, and as I walked out of the station it was absolutely throwing it down. As luck would have it, I managed to catch a taxi and asked the driver to take me to a hotel for the night, knowing full well that one of the lads already on the job had fixed me up with digs for the following day.

The taxi driver tried two or three different hotels, and found that they were either full up or closed for the night. In his exasperation, he happened to mention that a brand new Salvation Army hostel had just been built, and had only opened a couple of weeks earlier, and it was somewhat different from their ordinary run-of-the-mill hostels' in so far as half of it was made up of private rooms, completely separate from the homeless section, and he had heard from two or three people who had stayed there for a short time that they were quite smart.

It was only five minutes away from where we were, which as I was to find out later was the centre of Rochdale. There was nowhere else to go so I said I would give it a try for the night.

As it turned out, it was quite a smart place, the private rooms were a bit on the small side, but they all came with a sink, toilet and even more important on that particular winter's night, central heating. In fact, they were more or less on a par with what you would expect of a good two star hotel and to finish it off I had a right good night's sleep.

I was up bright and early the following morning and after a good wash and shave, I wandered around for a minute or two before I found the breakfast room, but I am sorry to say that it wasn't as private as the room had been.

It was an extremely large room with what looked to be a fairly large stainless steel kitchen with a serving hatch for passing the food through. This was situated at the far right hand corner of the breakfast room. Apart from this somewhat solid-looking corner, the rest of the existing walls were mostly made of glass, with numerous large window openers that were wide open. It must have been the closest I have ever come to walking into a bloody freezer, I really could not believe it. All this Shit in the name of God.

I decided to forget about it as I wouldn't be there for more than ten minutes. I approached the counter and ordered a coffee and a piece of toast, and for some reason I couldn't stop myself from referring to the open windows, and I would like them to please close them, to which the bloke answered that he wasn't allowed to it was the captain's orders.

While sitting there drinking my coffee, I had a good look around at the other people eating their breakfast, which by the law of averages, would be stone cold, if not freezing by the time they had eaten the other half.

The majority that were eating were mainly of an older type with half of them sounding as though they had very bad bronchitis and asthma. I really could not believe what I was seeing. It was while I was trying to get my head around the situation that a tall, fat, well dressed man who looked to be in his early forties walked in, and some of the old fellows said, 'Good morning, captain'.

I finished my coffee and was on my way out. As I came abreast of the captain I overheard him say to a couple of old chaps who were coughing their heads off, while at the same time gasping for breath, 'Come on, you two. Get a move on, you've been here more than half an hour!'

For me, hearing these words from someone like him, that begs the Government and more importantly the British public for their hard-earned money to help these people, made me snap, 'You fat bastard! What do you think you're doing to these poor people? They're nearly freezing to death in here and you won't allow them to close the fucking windows! What kind of pig are you? It must have taken a moment or two for his brain to take in what this mere mortal had just said to him.

With a red face, he answered that it was the Salvation Army's regulations that they remove their clientele to the street as quickly as possible so that the cleaners could get their work done, and if it was warm in the canteen they would take their time in going out.

That's when I said to him, 'How would you like to be put out in the street in this weather, being already half dead from bronchitis?'

Believe it or not, the words that came out of his fat mouth were, 'I am sorry sir but it is company policy, and I cannot do anything about it.'

From that day to this I have never given the Salvation Army one penny of my money and never will do, and neither should you after reading this. After all, there are many charities out there who would use your money far better than them in helping those of us who can't help ourselves.

The Asbestos Factory

When I arrived at Turner Bros. asbestos factory, which was better known in Greater Manchester as TBA, I couldn't believe my eyes, for want of a better expression. It was like walking into the Garden of Eden, the only difference being that the women were clothed, and there were a lot of overhead conveyor belts, making a hell of a noise. Nevertheless it looked to me as though it would be a very interesting job.

The foreman on the job was once again a little Irish man, believe it or not, and just for a change he was called Paddy.

Paddy, as it happened, was bald-headed, crinkle faced, and didn't wear his false teeth to work, but on top of all that he was hilarious, and a good boss.

He was one of those foremen who preferred not only to run the job, but also work alongside the lads where the manual work was concerned.

After showing me around the job, and what he wanted me to work on, he took me to see his landlord who fixed me up with a bed-sit in the same house as Paddy and a couple of other lads from the job.

Paddy and I paired up so he could show me the ropes for a couple of days, letting me get the hang of things. The main work consisted of dismantling, while at the same time replacing overhead conveyor belts. After a few days of working with him, I knew all the pedigrees of the lads who worked for our company.

There were, at that time, about ten of us on the job, plus two or three local lads that the firm had taken on for the duration of the contract. It turned out that the big day at the factory was a Friday when the girls finished work for the weekend at midday' and if for some reason you had forgotten it was Friday you would automatically be brought back to reality by seeing hundreds upon hundreds of young girls and women entering the factory with curlers in their hair, ready for the weekend on the town.

By that time in my life I thought I had seen everything, but nothing compared to this.

Most dinner times a few of the lads would go to the nearest pub for a beer and sandwich which was only two minutes walk from the factory gates, but all that changed on a Friday when the girls finished work, and like us, during the week, headed for the nearest pub. The weekend had just begun. God help Rochdale!

Just for a minute, try to visualize yourself and a few of your work mates sitting in a small, two-roomed pub, having a beer and a sandwich, and all of a sudden you can't move; you are completely surrounded by young girls, anywhere between sixteen and their early twenties with the majority of them drinking pints of beer, and at the same time swearing their heads off, which invariably got worse the more beer they drank.

On top of that, if you wanted to go to the toilet you had to somehow make your way through these crowds of half drunk women to the bar area in the far corner where the toilets were situated, and on your way there and back they would maul you – feeling your cobblers with exclamations like, 'Ee lad you've got a big un there,' or alternatively, 'Ee lad you couldn't do much for me with that, me 'usband's got a bigger one and he's no bloody good,' with them all roaring their heads off at your expense.

But I must admit that there was an upside to it, for while they were giving you a slagging, some of them would be pushing their tits up against you, or if they liked the look of you, would grab you on the way past and give you a kiss, with the rest of their friends feeling your rear end or anywhere else they fancied putting their hands.

One of the biggest problems that this caused in the North, and still does from what I can see, is that because of the power of the women, some of the wives are inclined to be promiscuous. Don't get me wrong, in fact I would go so far as to say I loved it, and probably always will do, but only as long as I don't end up marrying one of them.

By the way, you will get a better idea just how loose the women were in those times, by the fact that over a period of twelve years living in the North there are not enough fingers on my two hands to count the wives I have loaned one to, including a couple of instances where the husbands knew about it, including one who used to join us, and while I was giving her one, got his own enjoyment by having a J.Arthur Rank. Incidentally, I saw to this young lady on numerous occasions, and having her husband watching us was a real turn-on for all of us.

Let's get back to work, and all those beautiful women; in that particular era, the northern women were well known for their beauty, even though they were a bit rough around the edges, character-wise.

Lancashire Lasses

The first girl I had a date with after my arrival in Rochdale was one of the factory workers. She was what you would call half-caste, but did seem from her colour to have more white than black blood in her. At the time I started dating her she was 17, and absolutely gorgeous, full of life along with plenty of humour.

The first time I took her out for a drink, She informed me that I couldn't take her anywhere near the town centre as her boyfriend or one of his mates might see us, so we opted for a pub at the top end of the Spotland area' near to where my bed-sit was situated. It was called the Black Dog, and is still there to this day.

As was normal while out having a few drinks with a young lady, my first priority was to chat her up for going back to my digs at closing time, and I am glad to say that was where we ended up.

On entering the bed-sit there was no hesitation in her whatsoever when it came to taking her clothes off, and what that little lady didn't know about sex wasn't worth knowing. In no time she had my cock in her mouth – at that time in our great country's history, we referred to cock-sucking as 'giving you a gobble' – and the way that young lady performed the act on me, in my estimation, was as though she had done it from birth, as in a natural-born cocksucker, even to the point of swallowing my sperm, which she later told me she had been doing for her boyfriend for more than a year, and had grown to love the taste of it.

It was well past midnight before she left, and I have no doubt her lovely little bum must have been a bit on the sore side' as she sat down on the taxi seat!

My new girlfriend went by the name of Tracy, and as I was to find out later on in our friendship' her favourite sex act was a penis up her rear end, in fact she absolutely loved it, even to the point of me having to put my hand over her mouth as she was going over the top, to stop the other people in the house from hearing her screams as I pumped it into her.

Even though this happened many years ago, I can still picture in my mind that lovely off-white posterior sticking up in the air waiting for me to drive my hard cock into it, and the squeals that would invariably follow. The thought of it now is enough to give me a lob on!

I saw Tracy on and off for six months or so, and without any doubt I fell in love with, that young lady's rear end, which was quite amazing to me as it seems, in retrospect, that there was some love in me after all. Or was it lust? Over the first four or five months working at TBA I had dates with numerous women that worked there but none of them lasted very long, which didn't bother me in any way as I was still seeing Tracy, and none of the others had been a patch on her.

My drinking partner most of the time was Paddy who was always good company to be in, especially where the craic was concerned. Even though most of the girls liked

Paddy a lot, none of them seemed to fancy him sexually, plus it probably didn't help the situation that he never tried to tap them up, and nearly always forgot to put his false teeth in.

Tracy and I had decided, after the first half-a-dozen dates, to play it safe, owing to the fact that one of her boyfriend's mates had bumped into us having a drink together' but luckily for us, there were a crowd of us, and it was hard for his mate to say who, if anyone, was with her' It was just after that incident that we decided to meet at my bed-sit in future and have a few drinks there, along with a bit of the other.

Have you ever thought, especially those gentlemen in their late 50s and 60s, that when you were a lot younger, like 18 or 20 years of age, the law of averages says you will, at sometime, have sworn blind to your best mate that the girl you married would have to be a virgin on your wedding night. Just ask yourself how we would have all managed to marry virgins in that particular era, when you and your mates would probably go out every other night, and if not, every weekend, chasing the girls specifically to conquer that hopefully-still small hole between their legs. And if and when you managed it, that was one less virgin for your mates to marry, or you for that matter, unless of course you had fallen for her, God Forbid. And what about the other lads of a similar age to you and your mates who are doing the same thing as you are, up and down our great country every weekend, filling those little holes that used to belong to virgins? Logically speaking, how on earth could any of us expect to marry a virgin? Perhaps the only exception to the rule was the young chap that courted his girlfriend from the age of thirteen and never let her out of his sight until after taking her cherry on their wedding night.

I would say, in reality, that the chances in our era of marrying a virgin were the same as you had of being struck by lightning, but not quite. Concerning this day and age, you have as much chance of marrying one as being struck twice by lightning' while you are sitting in a bar with no windows' I rest my case!

I had been working up north for more than six months when I met the girl that was to change my life. Her name was Ann, she was an extremely good-looking girl and from what I could find out about her, she was one of those, and there are always a few, who didn't knock on with every Tom, Dick or Harry. For those of you that don't understand the expression 'knock on' it means even to this day in the north of England, that the girl in question would go out with lots of men, and drop her pants around her ankles on a regular basis. I am glad to say Ann didn't. In fact, I had to chat her up for a couple of weeks before she would even consider going out with me.

She was also the first girl that I had gone out with that was similar in height to me. I had always been inclined to go for smaller women up until then, please don't ask me why, because I have no bloody idea, but that I am glad to say was where the similarity ended.

She had everything, a lovely figure, nice-shaped breasts, nice legs and a beautiful Arse. What more could a man ask for? And you can rest assured there was no shortage of local lads chasing after her' trying to get into her knickers.

I had taken her out a dozen times or more before I managed, with a lot of persuasion, to get her to agree to come back to my bedsit for a coffee.

By this time I knew that she liked me a lot, and it was probably the right time to push her a bit to drop her knickers, and I know you won't believe what I am going to tell you, but after successfully getting her to part with them and my dick ready to invade, I couldn't get it into her. She was a bloody virgin! I just thank God that at that particular moment in time there was a jar of Vaseline at hand, and after a bit of perseverance I managed to give her a good and enjoyable introduction to the world of sex for the next three hours or more! She ended up staying the night, and arranged with her friends to tell her parents she had stayed with them.

From then on we were inseparable' and God help me, I was in love for the first time in my life, and at the same time had got one over on that "Struck by lightning" in fact, and in retrospect, I should have reported it to the Guinness Book of Records. To top it off, she was 22, and that in itself had to be a bloody record for Rochdale.

Merthyr Tydfil

Shortly after meeting her, the boss sent me down to Merthyr Tydfil in Wales to give the lads who were already there a hand to finish off a job that could only be done at night' so as not to cause any inconvenience to factory production during the working day.

Each night we had to go in and dismantle ex-amount of over-head conveyor belts, and replace them with new before the workers arrived at 8am.

The Welsh drinking hours in those days were almost non-existent' but never the less one or two of the landlords would open their back doors most of the day, for night workers' with I believe the full knowledge of the local police, with whom on occasion I had the privilege of having a few pints, and a good laugh!

Thank the Lord' the job was finished in ten days and I was winging my way back to Rochdale and my one true love.

Since meeting Ann I had cut down on the times that I met Tracy, as much as I adored her, knowing full well in my own mind that if I carried on as usual it would only be a matter of time before someone let the cat out of the bag in front of Ann.

As it happened I had nothing to worry about where Tracy was concerned, even though we had been going together for a good many months.

When I broke the news to her about the new love of my life, lo and behold, her boyfriend had just asked her to marry him, and she had accepted and decided to stop playing away, our last night of course being the exception, which needless to say was fantastic!

My Home Coming

After three months of going together, Ann became pregnant' and without the consent of her Parents' who were totally opposed to the marriage' we decided to go to Birmingham and get married in the Registrars' Office on Broad Street, On our arrival in Birmingham, my Brother Sean managed to get us a pleasant little bed-sit in Edgbaston' and shortly after that we were married.

Less than a week after settling into our bed-sit, I managed to get a job in Birmingham town centre with one of my previous employers, Brightside Heating and Ventilation Co, who I had worked for all over the country in the past. The work was on the then new ATV studios being built off Broad Street, behind the Registrars' Office the same one where I had been married.

The general foreman for the company on site went by the name of Sam and right from the start we got on like a house on fire. This particular job was somewhat different from the others. Instead of just installing Heating and

Ventilation as was normal they had now branched out into sprinkler systems, which made for a lot of work to get through. Needless to say there was always plenty of overtime available, which I needed more than ever, with a new wife and a child on the way. I also knew that, because of the good work I had done for them, and being the conscientious worker that they knew I was in the past, they would more than likely keep me on the longest; I had landed on my feet once again!

It was just after starting on the television centre that Birmingham Housing Department offered us a council house in Castle Bromwich, on one of the new overspill housing estates.

Our First Council House

Things were certainly beginning to shape up for us. Castle Vale estate to the working classes in those days was like moving to a new planet; there were trees, green areas, and new schools for the kids, new modern pubs, and even a small forest where you could take a nice walk. In fact where the wife and I were concerned, it was fantastic, and without any doubt it was a far better environment to bring your kids up than the centre of Birmingham.

At the time of moving in' my son Stuart had been born, and our second was on the way. When our second child was born, we named her Margaret after my mother-in-law, who I could never get on with. On top of that, I didn't particularly like the name of Margaret, and had only agreed because of the pressure put on me by my wife.

I myself called my daughter Maggie from day one which I liked far more, and on top of that I knew my mother-in-law hated the name. Who said it's nice to be nice?

The only downside to my job was the travelling to and from work every day, especially in the mornings. If you missed a bus, you would have to wait for another half hour or more, for the next one to show up, but I suppose it was a small price to pay to live in the countryside.

Another good side to living where we did was the fact that it wasn't far from where my brother Jimmy and his wife Georgina lived, and who were also the proud owners of their own semi-detached house – which was almost unheard of in those days, as far as the working classes were concerned – so it enabled us to have a night out with them every now and then in Castle Bromwich itself, which was far more lively than the estate where we lived. I had been working at the TV studio going on three months when my brother Jack lost his job at a small building company that he had worked for since doing his national service, and although he had worked there for many years he received no redundancy pay or anything else for that matter.

To cut a long story short, I had a chat with my friend' and immediate boss, and he gave him a job as a fitter's mate, working on the new sprinkler system at the studio. Our Jack had only been there two or three weeks when the firm started to send him on contracts out of town, which I believe he enjoyed at that particular time in his life! After all, he had been married for a good many years by then, so I am quite sure as lovely a person as his wife Maureen was – and still is I might say – he was more than ready for a break (as in distance makes the heart grow fonder!) My job, on the other hand lasted in excess of twelve Months, and towards the end I was offered the opportunity of staying on for a further three months doing any maintenance necessary, which was part of the company's contract with ATV. Even better, it was a seven-day-a-week job.

It was the kind of job where you were your own boss, with the main part of that job being tours of the property at regular intervals looking for leaks etc.

It was, as it turned out, quite educational in as far as it gave me an insight into how TV studios operate, concerning the making of soap operas and numerous other programmes.

One particular programme that I used to watch live, every Sunday afternoon, was Bob Monkhouse making the famous 'Golden Shot' and it was far better viewing from where I and one or two other maintenance men stood in our overalls' than it was sat at home

The 'Golden Shot' audience, for half-an-hour before it was beamed on to your television set at home, would be entertained by none other than Bob Monkhouse himself, as he really was, that being a stand up comedian' and presenting us with his real jokes! the same that he uses on his club tours, with most of them being a bit near the bone.

In fact, until the first time I saw him in action live in the studio I used to think he was a bit on the smarmy side, as seen in the 'Golden Shot'. However, folks, take my word for it, as comedians go, Bob Monkhouse must have been one of the greatest comedians that this country has ever produced.

Back to the show! By the end of the half hour the audience were roaring their heads off, and that is the moment when it was beamed out to the public, showing the audience in the studio in a right happy mood, and willing to watch a somewhat boring programme for an hour.

By the time my job came to an end there was very little work to be had in the Midlands, or anywhere else for that matter. The slump had set in. I did manage to get a bit of pipefitting work here and there for a few weeks, and on one occasion was daft enough to take my brother Sean with me as my mate. To say he drove me up the fucking wall is putting it mildly!

I do, in retrospect, believe' that' that was the turning point in my life where my grey hair was concerned. God bless you Sean! By the way, I have just entered your lovely wife Maureen for the Nobel Peace Prize, as in my opinion if anyone deserves it she does!

CHAPTER TEN

My First Winter In Rochdale

At around the time that the work began to get scarce in Birmingham, I was offered a job by my father-in- law with a transport company he helped to run in Rochdale, along with a new council flat he had managed to find for us, but the offer wouldn't last forever.

After talking it over with my wife we decided to give it a try. By the way my wife had been on my back for the previous twelve months or more to move up to Rochdale where she had felt sure her father would be able to find me a job, so needless to say after my agreeing to accept her father's offer she was over the moon.

On our arrival, we moved into a Brand new three bedroomed flat in an area called Ashfield Valley, thus began my new life in the north of England.

And for as long as I live I will never forget the day I started work at Rochdale's largest transport carriers (Wilkinsons Transport) It was at ten to seven on a winter's morning, and bloody freezing!

Waiting at the entrance to the company was my father-in-law. We will call him Tommy for now. When I reached the entrance I really could not believe what I was seeing, and, but for the fact that I was skint, I would have told him, in no uncertain way, to shove his job, flat and all, right up his fucking arse!

Just try to imagine for a moment, that you are walking up a narrow cobbled street, the only white thing visible being the frosted cobbles' and if that wasn't bad enough you could not see more than a couple of feet in front of you owing to the dense smog! And added to that, the street being one of those that you have never seen before in your life, and all of a sudden you stumble into what I can only describe as a large black hole in a wall, which I later realized was the entrance into the warehouse. At this entrance all you can see in front of you is a massive cloud of what I later found out to be diesel fumes which actually began to choke you before you entered the place.

After entering into this cloud of diesel smoke and fumes, and coming out to what seemed to be the other side, you would just be able to make out with the help of straining your eyes somewhat, a large U-shaped wooden loading bay, with between thirty and forty extremely large diesel vans, with most of them looking as though they would be unsafe to drive. At the same time as you saw the vans, you couldn't help but notice the massive clouds of black smoke coming from the exhaust pipes of each and every one of them. I later found out that the drivers were revving their diesel engines up, and trying to get them warm enough to set off once their wagon had been loaded by the deckhands. Behind them on the bay areas were twenty or more men with what you could only call sack trucks, actually running backwards and forwards loading the wagons, in some cases to the roof, and at the same time dressed as though they were taking a hike up Mount

Everest, including the hat and scarf covering their nose and mouth. I know for a fact that on occasions, because of the bad visibility we had to work in, that some of the truck pushers would actually crash into one another while going in and out of the vans. This kind of accident normally happened when one or more of the truckers took their mind off the job for a minute or two while shouting to the driver of the van they were loading, and telling him in the finest Queen's English, that if he didn't turn his fucking engine off, now that it had warmed up, he would go down there and break his fucking neck!

The drivers, on the other hand, sat in their cabs with their windows closed while they were being loaded, so only got a minimum of fumes in their guts.

I remember to this day the first impression that came into my mind on seeing this disgusting abuse of my fellow workers, apart of course from the total disgust I felt for the owners, and the powers that be for allowing such a violation of human rights.

But getting back to the overall picture that was imprinted in my mind in the first instance when I entered the place, it was as though I had been transported back a hundred years to the plight of the working masses in the Dickensian era, when they forced little children up chimneys to clean them, and the other monstrous jobs the working class were forced to perform for a slice of bread, and that picture I am sorry to say will stay with me for the rest of my days.

By ten o'clock each day, the wagons would be loaded and out on the road, then you would have your breakfast break, but you would only be able to eat if there was any space left in your body that wasn't full of diesel fuel. I must admit that after a few days I got used to it, and a couple of weeks after that I started a local branch of the Union, The Transport and General Workers' Union. What a load of bloody tossers they turned out to be!

By the way the ventilation in that warehouse was one of a kind. In fact, I would go so far as to say it was unique, in so far as from years before I worked there, and until this day, I have never seen the likes.

The roof on this property ran the full length of it, which would have been a minimum of 150 to 200 yards in length, made of asbestos panels and in the standard sloping design of the day. The only difference with this particular roof was when you looked up at it you could see the sky, but only after the wagons had departed and the diesel smoke had cleared sufficiently.

As most of you will be aware, a standard roof is two-sided, with both sides running up at angles until they join at what is called an apex. The difference in the construction off this roof was that the last asbestos panels on each side of what should have been the apex, had been left off, or removed to make what the management referred to as a 'natural ventilation system'.

One or two of the downsides of this type of ventilation, apart from being freezing, was the fact' and you are probably aware of it – is that the rain in the winter in the North of England never stops. When a downpour of rain met the black diesel smoke and fumes, or at least what was left of it, after the docking staff had had their lungs filled, it had turned to black rain by the time it had hit the cobbles below.

On top of this, they had constructed half a dozen sewer holes running down the centre of the cobbled floor, for the full length of the warehouse, with an assortment of grills covering them. It was in case one of the workers might get washed away, probably because if one of the lads disappeared into one of these holes they wouldn't be able to spare the time to fish him out. In those days, especially where that company was concerned, it would have been cheaper for them to replace him off the dole queue, than rescue him!

The standard hours that went with the job were 7am until 7pm, five days a week, with Saturday morning thrown in if you wished. On top of that, the wages were a minimum of 30% more than anywhere else in Rochdale, so in truth for as bad as I found the conditions in my workplace I nonetheless owed my father-in-law a thank you for getting me the job. In fact, at that particular time, there was a waiting list for workers wanting employment there, and plenty of them.

Tommy, my father-in-law, was a big man of at least six feet or a little more, with hands the size of shovels, and the physique to go with it, and not an ounce of fat on him. Going by what I found out later, he came from a family of more than twenty kids, and there's me thinking I had had a hard time when I was young. Compared to him I was brought up in a bloody holiday camp. I think I managed, with a lot of perseverance to stay in that job for two or three years, and managed somehow or other to buy a new townhouse, on mortgage of course, but I was only able to manage it because of the kind of wages I earned.

By this time my young son and daughter were growing up and money was tight. The majority of what we earned went on the mortgage on our new house. In fact, it got to the point, where the only sensible thing to do was to sell our property and move to a terraced house, thus cutting our mortgage in half which would leave us a small profit out of the townhouse sale, which would then give me a chance to go into some kind of business of my own.

The million dollar question at the time was 'would the wife agree? My biggest problem where my wife was concerned was that at that particular time, she only had one thing in her mind, and that was to go forwards not backwards, how she expected that to happen in the situation we found ourselves in is anybody's guess.

Just imagine for a moment, that you were to find yourself in a similar situation to myself. There's yourself' your wife, two young children and last, but not least, the dog.

Your wife works evening shifts in a cotton mill and earns a decent wage, and you work your arse off 65 hours a week! Week in and week out, and earned a lot more than your standard Rochdale worker.

You suddenly wake up one morning, at your usual time of 5.30am, in order to start work at 7 am, but unlike the other five mornings you get up to go to work, you suddenly think to yourself, 'What the fuck am I doing with my life?'

Over a cup of tea and a cigarette, which by the way is the only things you have time for, before starting work at seven, you weigh up the pros and cons of your, and your family's future, if you carry on the way you are going.

You then come to your decision. After all, at the end of the day, you are the main breadwinner in the house, and as such are entitled to the main say in the future of your family. By the way, your decision doesn't come easily, and on top of that, you know that at the end of the day there is a fair chance that it would widen the rift that already existed between you and your wife. What would you do?

I don't know what you would have done about it, but I can tell you what I decided to do, and without hesitation did so!

I gave my dear wife an ultimatum, either we moved together as a family to a terraced house, or I would leave her, and move back to Birmingham.

I moved back to Birmingham! By the way my wife was aware of where I was staying in Brum, which as it happened was with my younger brother.

It was two or three weeks later that I received a phone call from her agreeing to do what I wished' for the sake of the children who needed their father' and she also missed me-the latter I believed at the time' was a load of cobblers.

On my return to Rochdale' we sold up and moved to a very nice terraced house near Syke Common, where now after working all week we had a few bob in our pockets' plus a few hundred quid in the bank' and even better I had now left the black hole that I had worked in for the past two years or more, under duress I might say' for the light of day!

Decorating

It was around this time that I met a couple of decorators in my new local "The Tanners Arm's" on Whitworth Road.
At the time they were on what was called the 715 certificate' which enabled the owner to work as a self employed person' exempt from paying tax for the first twelve months

The main problem for me' was what kind of work would be open to me if I acquired one of these certificates, with my past experience being limited to pipe fitting and steel erecting, for which there was very little call for' where I lived.

One of my new mates called Henry told me that if I was willing to take a chance and a low wage for a little time, he would get me started on the housing estate that he and Mick, his mate, were both working on at that time. It was in a place called Middleton and he would be able to teach me to decorate sufficiently well in a couple of weeks, so as to enable me to bluff my way until I had enough experience to earn good wages.

The only downside to his offer was the possibility of me not being able to adapt to this new trade, and when you consider that in those days most painters and decorators had to serve a five-year apprenticeship, the possibility of me making a balls-up was very high.

From the age of fifteen, I had always enjoyed work, and still do, but another talent that I had seemed to pick up' or perhaps without knowing it' it was in fact part of my make-up' was the ability to learn, with relative ease, more or less any job I had put my mind to, but even so I knew that this one would be a very hard nut to crack! And if I failed I would be up to my neck' in shit!

Greater Manchester Council

At that particular time in Greater Manchester the local councils were stripping off and totally redecorating whole housing estates, both inside and out, and couldn't get enough paperhangers for love nor money. Painters by the way were ten-a-penny.

The unofficial name for a painter in Greater Manchester, in those days and still to this day, is a tosher! On the other hand the nickname for a paperhanger is 'slinger' no doubt derived from the well-known word, gunslinger, which came down to how fast you could draw your scissors from the side leg pocket of your overalls for cutting the paper. In essence, it did in fact, give the illusion, that you were drawing a six-gun, and the faster a slinger could draw his scissors from its holster, the more paper he could cut, hence the more money he would make!

With the help of my two mates four weeks after starting I was making a decent wage! And after six months, I was known as one of the fastest slingers on Site, and was earning some bloody good money.

CHAPTER ELEVEN

Back To The Old Ways

The work was drying up on the job I had started on with Henry and Mick, so Henry, and a lad called Derrick and myself started work for a different decorating company who were opening a new site, and paying better prices per dwelling.

Henry and I teamed up as a double act, with me going in front doing the ceilings, and Henry following behind doing the walls.

We always started early in the mornings if possible, because we both believed in the old saying, 'The early bird catches the worm' always knowing that provided we got a good morning in, we more times than not ended the day making a good wage.

A lot of the houses we had to decorate still had their council tenants living in them, in which case we were paid a higher rate for our work, because in most cases the houschold furniture slowed us down.

On one particular morning as I entered one house, the woman who let me in was quite attractive, probably in her early to middle thirties, and on the face of it she seemed to be quite friendly.

It was while I was taking my gear upstairs to start on the ceilings, that she mentioned that her daughter was still in bed and wouldn't get up, and could I manage to do the ceiling while she was lying in bed, and that her daughter wouldn't bother me as she was fast asleep, With this remark, she smiled and put her tongue out at me in a little girl sort of way. 'Well, you had better be off then, but I'll know if any naughty things happen because I will hear the springs going!'

I was halfway through slinging the ceiling, when I happened to look down at the sleeping girl, and at that very moment she turned over onto her back, with the quilt covering her slipping down below her breasts. For a moment, to say I was traumatized would have been putting it mildly. Well, can you just imagine yourself papering someone's ceiling, and all of a sudden you look down, and see a lovely pair of 17 or 18-year-old tits standing up on their own in all their glory? What would you do? And more importantly, what could I do under the circumstances, but carry on and finish the ceiling! I was just slinging the last-but one length of woodchip when I heard a scream from the girl followed by something like, 'Who the fuck are you?' as she jumped out of the bed, brushing one of her breasts that seemed to have a big gob of paste on it. By God, her tits were beautiful, and on top of that, the fact that I hadn't had a bit of spare for quite a while didn't help.

Anyone who is or has been married over a period of a few years, after knocking two or three kids out of the wife, knows well enough that the breasts your wife originally had, and you had lovingly fondled, and probably sucked the nipples of, when you were courting her, are no more, and this is most certainly true if your wife has breast-fed.

So, back to those 17 or 18-year-old 'Bristol Cities' that had not yet been suckled. It would be enough to send you around the twist, and on top of that, I did manage to get a glimpse of her lovely little arse. You know the type, with no stretch marks on! In a flash she slipped into her dressing gown, and ran towards the bedroom door like a bat out of hell, just as her mother entered the room laughing her head off.

'Annie she said, I called you twice, telling you to get your bum out of bed, because the decorators were coming in, and you told me to bugger off, so it serves you right. Anyway, he's not too bad a sight to wake up to, and from what I have seen of some of the fellows you have woken up to in the past, most of them were far worse. Anyway, I've made you a brew, it's in the kitchen.

As Annie was going past her mother to get out of the room I shouted to her, 'Hey, luv! Could I have a replay? On hearing this her mother burst out laughing, and I will leave you to guess what Annie's answer was.

Because we worked as self-employed, and had to make our own money – as in no production, no wages our dinner breaks were normally twenty to thirty minutes, maximum. In other words just sufficient time to eat a sandwich, drink a cup of tea, and have a cigarette, full stop.

As it happened, that particular day was the exception to the rule, and I ended up spending an hour or more chatting the mother and daughter up, to have a night out with me and my mate at the weekend. By this time, Annie the daughter had woken up and was now laughing about the incident, and mentioned that her mother got great enjoyment from putting her into embarrassing situations.

It was obvious after spending a bit of time chatting with them that they acted more like sisters than mother and daughter, and there was no doubt that they thought a lot about one another.

It didn't take a lot of persuasion to get them to agree to meet me and my mate at one of their local pubs on the following Friday night.

It seemed that Annie had a good job working three days a week in one of the big stores in Manchester, and I had caught her on one of her days off. Before I left to do my next house of ceilings, the mother invited me for a brew and a chat the next day, at around lunchtime, which I was more than happy to accept.

The mother's name was Patricia, but she preferred to be called Trish, and by this time I knew I was on a sure thing. The next day I started work an hour earlier than usual, and really went to town on my slinging, just in case I was a bit late back from lunch, which I thought there was a fair possibility! The previous day, I had got the feeling that she was attracted to me, and if my past experiences was anything to go on, I was almost certain she was a goer!

When I arrived, the first thing I noticed was that she had made herself far more attractive than she had been the previous day, a little makeup, a dress that showed off a very nice figure. In fact, all round, she looked good enough to eat.

I don't know about you, but I have often come across women that look far more sexy, and have far more attractive figures than a lot of women that are fifteen years younger, and are normally far better company in bed and out. While I had my sandwich and a cup of tea, we had a right good chat, mainly about everyday things, that eventually led to her talking about her own personal life, including the bringing up of her daughter for the last 13 or 14 years on her own.

She had met her husband at a local dance just before she was sixteen, and became pregnant with Annie.

Although she thought quite a lot of her boyfriend at that particular time, she wasn't sure she wanted to marry him, and the pregnancy itself had been an unforeseen accident due solely to too much drink. When she realized she was going to have a baby, her mother and father persuaded her to have nothing to do with the boyfriend, and they would help her bring the baby up, which she was over the moon about.

While all this was going on, she began to hear stories about her boyfriend knocking on with other young girls in the area, which after making a few enquiries herself, she found to be true. After finding out about the kind of chap the father of her baby really was, she took her parents advice and told him to get on his bike. Once the baby was born, the boyfriend was never away from her house, mainly bringing presents for both her and the baby, and telling her every chance that he got, that she and the baby were the only loves in his life. By the time Annie was six months old she had agreed to marry him for the sake of the baby, who she knew he adored, and would do anything for. To this day she regrets ever having done so, as he turned out to be a real shit.

They had been married for twelve months when he buggered of with a local Nancy-boy, never to be seen again, and from that day to this she had sworn never to remarry.

Over the next few years she had turned down numerous offers of marriage, she then started to tell me about her sex life with her husband, and some of the things he used to do to her, and sometimes using violence towards her if she refused.

One of his favourite sex games was to tie her naked, face down, to the dining room table and rape her bum, but this usually happened after he had used a leather belt on the cheeks of her arse before hand. He had told her that when he heard her squeals while using the belt that it gave him a hard-on' a rock hard one!

When I asked her about the effect it had had on her, she did admit that after two or three times she began to enjoy it, and that there had actually come a time when she did in fact, look forward to it.

By this time, as you can no doubt imagine, the graphic descriptions she had just given me of her sex life had turned me on to the point where my cock was also rock-hard.

By the time she had finished, we were sitting on her settee, with my left arm over her shoulder stroking one of her breasts through her dress, while my right hand was under her dress massaging her thighs, and there was no doubt in my mind from the way she had started kissing me, that she was more than ready for what was now standing upright in my trousers. By the way, I still didn't wear underpants at that time, and very rarely do nowadays.

I was to be proved right when five minutes later she unzipped my trousers, and took my rock-hard penis into her mouth, followed by little noises coming from her as she moved the knob-end of my penis backwards and forwards between her soft pink lips.

She had only had it in her mouth for three or four minutes when my trousers were off. Only seconds after that, her dress and knickers came off, leaving her with only her nylons and suspender belt. Two seconds later my rock-hard dick was buried up to the hilt in her vagina, with the living room curtains still wide open for all the world to see. Needless to say, my wages were a bit on the low side that week, and I was completely knackered.

Come Friday, my mate Henry had a date elsewhere, so another mate of mine who had started on this particular site with Henry and me – that I might have mentioned in passing – called Derek, agreed to make up the foursome.

We met them at a very large pub near Blakely where we found them waiting for us when we entered the lounge area. They were supping two glasses of white wine, and

there were two pints of bitter waiting for us. Now, if that's not a good start to a first date, I don't know what is.
It didn't take Derek long before he had them laughing their heads off, followed by a few more drinks, and a bit of rock'n'roll.

When we arrived back at their place, they gave us a beer and decided to change their clothes for something more comfortable. We did try to talk them into not bothering to change into anything else, as we would prefer them without anything on, to which Trish replied, 'Ah, but you don't know what we are going to change into, and who knows? You just might like it!

While they were upstairs changing, Derek asked me if I thought they might go for changing partners, as he wanted to fuck both of them. After talking about it for a few minutes, we worked out a strategy, and decided to try it on. We knew that by the law of averages, we would end up in the girls' separate bedrooms, mainly of course because there was only one settee in the living room.

We decided that when we had had our way with our prospective young ladies, whoever was finished first would make his way to the bathroom, and in reality come into the others bedroom by mistake, and take it from there.

It was at the same time that we had settled on our scheme that the girls appeared, and oh what a sight for sore eyes! I am getting a hard-on just thinking back to that night! and I would swear on a stack of bibles that I can see them now, as clear as if they were stood in front of me.

Two lovely girls, dressed identically, in what I can only describe as Baby-Doll Nighties, (they were the in things in those times) just high enough to see the lower half of both vaginas, which I am happy to say also gave us a glimpse of a small part of their pink lips that weren't quite camouflaged with their masses of brown hair, and if that wasn't enough they had finished it off with white stockings and suspenders.

In the few seconds that it took my brain to take it all in, you could have stuck a Union Jack on the end of my cock. In fact it was so hard it was hurting, and to top it off, they did a little twirl in front of us, and the sight of their lovely little bums made my cock ache even more.

We had our clothes off in less than twenty seconds, and moved in for the kill. I managed to catch Trish from behind, one arm around her waist and the other massaging her lovely tits, while at the same time my now-aching, rock-hard cock was stuck between the cheeks of her now wriggling little arse. Trish didn't need telling what I wanted, as she had already had it in the same place two or three times over the previous few days, orgasming every time, while at the same time squealing like a banshee.

By this time I had manoeuvred her to the back of the settee, which from previous experience I now knew was the ideal height needed for a comfortable insertion into her sexy little bum. It really got me going when she let out a squeal as my knob-end popped into her, and you can rest assured of one thing – that young lady loved my cock filling up her rear end, which was no doubt brought about when she had been forced to endure' and later after plenty of the same' from her Bi-sexual husband' had realized she could not do without it.

At the same time that I was pulling out of Trish's anus, her daughter was just climbing off Derek's lap, where he had obviously given her a good time, if the noises coming from both of them was anything to go by. There was us, less than half an hour earlier, trying to set them up for a swap over, and we had already managed to have sex with them in each other's presence. Who knows? Perhaps it was a family tradition!

I decided there and then to tell her that Derek fancied her and would love to have sex with her, to which she didn't seem surprised in the least, and in fact said she would like that, but it would depend on her daughter agreeing.

She then mentioned that her daughter had fancied me since the day I had dropped the wallpaper paste on to those lovely tits of hers, so she would now take her daughter into the kitchen to get us a drink, and see what she thought about it.

By this time, I was more than ready for a cigarette, and asked Derek for one of his.

While we were sat there waiting for our drinks, Derek suddenly burst out, 'Bloody hell, Charlie! Where do you find them? Most of those I have pulled around here have been as rough as old boots.'

As I bent down to get a light from him for my cigarette, I told him in a whisper what I had said to Trish about swapping, and with a bit of luck she might be having a word with Annie right then.

It was after telling Derek about what might be going on in the kitchen, that I shouted to Trish that we were sat here dying for a drink, and when were our lovely waitresses coming to serve us?

The only answer I received was a roar of laughter followed by Trish shouting, 'You two be quiet! We are well worth waiting for, so count yourselves lucky!

Can you just imagine for a minute sitting on a settee, and two beautiful young ladies coming out of the kitchen carrying two bottles of beer, dressed only in white nylons and suspenders' while walking towards you with their lovely bushy vaginas and their pink lips slightly open? What would you do? Down I went and my tongue went straight into Trish's. It was bloody fantastic and I decided, there and then, that there was no way on this earth, as much as I wanted to fuck her daughter that Derek was going to get into her little red-hot pepper-pot before I did. With that, I said I would have my beer later, and pulled Trish up the stairs to her bedroom with Annie shouting after us, 'Mum! I thought we were changing over, and with Trish answering, 'Give us a half hour love!

It had turned five o'clock in the morning when I arrived home. Thankfully my wife was snoring her head off, and I managed to slip in beside her, without disturbing her.

The next morning, if you could call it that, I told her that me and some of my mates had ended up drunk in a club in Manchester, and had fallen asleep.

I think she only just believed me. Incidentally, we did swap partners before the night was over, and no disrespect to Annie with the lovely tits but she wasn't a patch on her mother "Some time's they say that you can get a better tune from an older fiddle"

I would just like a moment of your time to enlighten you folk out there about my sex life at home. In my case at that time it was nonexistent, owing to the wife once again being off it. And I would also like to mention to anyone reading this story, especially the women, that when your old man has got a hard-on, and you have got another one of your many headaches, that hard-on will eventually find another entrance to accommodate it' elsewhere! That was exactly what mine had been doing!

It was to be another three months before we completed our work on that particular estate and although I had other affairs with two other younger women, I never found any of them to be a patch on Trish.

Trish and I stayed friends and lovers for a good many years, right up until the time she met a nice man in his early 50s with plenty of money. In fact, if I remember correctly, he owned a very well known Manchester building company, and after a few months of going out together he asked Trish to marry him. I am very glad to say she accepted, and as far as I know they lived happily ever after, well I most certainly hope they did.

In between working for big companies on council housing estates, most of them being in the Greater Manchester area, I started to take on work for smaller builders, and some of them actually came knocking on my front door offering me work, as by then I had a good name, both in workmanship and reliability.

It was at that time that I decided to take on one or two of the local lads to help me out, the agreement always being, if they didn't put a good day's work in, they would be up the road, rapido!.

As it happened, I had started off right where workers were concerned. After one or two up the road, it was only the grafters that came to work for me, and they were always paid well above the odds.

There was one particular builder that had started to give me plenty of work around the Rochdale area. They were mainly terraced houses that he had totally renovated from top to bottom, and I would decorate them inside and out for him, with a guaranteed first class finish.

I was just in the process of finishing one of his houses for him when he asked me if I would be interested in decorating a row of twelve houses, or would it be too big a job for me? Thank God, I had never come across a job that was too big for me since the day I left school. I told him I was interested, and arranged to meet him the next day to have a look at them, and sort him out a decent price.

When I met him on site the next day I could see that his workmen were still working on site, with the work seeming to be concentrated on the last three Houses. I spent the next couple of hours or more checking the houses out, and making a snag list of what the builder needed to do in order to be ready for the decorators.

CHAPTER TWELVE

A good decorator can always cover up a multiple of sins for the builder, but in order to give a good price you had to let the builder know what you couldn't cover up, at breakfast time, which was around ten o'clock. The charge hand on the site, who I had got to know pretty well over the past twelve months invited me to the café with him and the lads for a bit of breakfast, plus it would give me and him a chance to discuss the ins and outs of the job.

When we entered the café, he found us an empty corner table away from the work lads, and we got down to business. Of course, the main items were the snagging jobs, and time element. By the way from the first house I had decorated in the past for his boss, I had always seen him right for a back hander, which insured no hold-up in my work schedule where his snagging was concerned, and any other bits of help that I might need like lifting, moving materials, etc, which at the end of the day could save me a lot of labour, on a job this size.

During our conversation, the charge hand informed me that his boss had a problem with the finishing time on his contract, with the housing company who owned the properties, and stood to lose a lot of money if he didn't hand them over on the date that was on the contract, which in fact made it better for me, and my pricing.

I knew by this time that it was 90% certain that even if my price was a little on the high side I would get the job, if only for the fact that he could rely on me for speed and a first class finish, of these two reasons he was more than well aware of from the previous work I had done for him. Needless to say, after receiving this information from his charge hand, I put in a high price, but telling him at the same time, that if he could wait for another five or six weeks, which was the normal waiting time for this kind of work from any small decorating company, I could do it for a much lower price. That would also give me sufficient time to catch up with my private work, which on the whole was far more lucrative than doing work for builders, and to top that off you were usually paid cash in the hand, which, in turn, cut out any problems you might have with your cash flow.

The builder, I am glad to say, accepted the price, but only on one condition and that was that I had to undertake, and he wanted it in writing, that I would have the twelve houses ready for turning over to the housing association in five weeks, or would pay a penalty. If I remember correctly, that was on the high side, no doubt to help him at the end of the day with his penalty, if it wasn't completed on time, and a further stipulation was that I must have men on site the following morning.

Five weeks, twelve houses. Thinking about it afterwards I must have been fucking crackers. Each house needed a primer, undercoat, and gloss finish on all the woodwork inside and out, including doors and radiators, wood-chipped ceilings throughout the house, finished with two coats of emulsion, with all walls finished in patterned papers.

To say it was a challenge was to understate it, but I am glad to say that at that time in my life I was an egotistical bastard, and that is putting it mildly. Never the less, apart from working full speed ahead, seven days a week, plus evenings, it was the only thing that got me through, and I finished the work with two days to spare. To say my builder friend was happy wasn't in it. In fact, he took all the lads who had worked on the job, his and mine, for a real piss-up, that lasted most of the afternoon, and cost him a small fortune.

I can't remember how much profit I made out of the job, but it was a hell of a lot, and I decided to take the wife and kids for a ten day cruise on the QE2 which for some strange reason I had always wanted to do. I think perhaps, in retrospect, it was probably because it was normally only rich people who could afford to sail on it in those days.

With new clothes for the family, top class of course, plus dinner suit and fancy dresses for me and the wife, it cost me well in excess of £3,000 and would have cost a lot more if I hadn't made a deal with the bar manager to pay him, cash in the hand, every couple of days rather than put it on our room tab, at a discount of 50%. That, of course, went straight into his pocket. What fool ever said that we lived in a straight world?

I will never forget attending our first evening meal. It was the same protocol every evening of the week. As you entered the dining room it resembled something that I had only seen the equal of in grand old movies, this Included the glittering Chandeliers. It was out of this world, and I have been to many beautiful, expensive restaurants both here and abroad over the years. Up to date, I have never seen one that could lick the boots of the QE2.

The moment you walked through the dining room door you were met by a fancy waiter who would, once again, remind you of a butler from an old movie. He would offer you an aperitif, and then lead you to your table, which would have all your individual names on fancy, designed cards.

The menu, and you won't get your head around this was ten courses, with the main course and many of the other courses being of a large selection. Who, in God's name, could possibly eat a ten course meal?

It didn't take me long to find out that a large percentage of the people in the dining room were well overweight, and more or less spent most of their time travelling around the world on the QE2, solely for the food, and the massive portions. I don't believe for the whole time I was on the liner I ever saw anyone under sixteen stone, and many, many, many more were in the 20 and 30 stone category. It was a glutton's paradise.

It was shortly after my QE2 trip that I decided to sell our terraced house and move up market a little. After a bit of looking around, I came across a lovely large Victorian property that was in excess of five times the value of my terraced house, and settled for that, which made the wife a little happier. My decorating business was flourishing, but

I knew deep down that to make a lot of money I would have to somehow get into the building trade.

My chance finally came when the Government brought out housing grants for certain run-down areas, mainly Asian.

It was around that time that I had become quite friendly with an Asian lad who was one of the few educated ones in his particular area, and was well thought-off by the local Asian Community, to the point where Rochdale Council and his own people used him as an interpreter.

One day when I called at his shop for a packet of cigs, and was enjoying a few minutes chat with him, he brought up the subject of the new grant systems in that area, informing me that the few grant jobs that had been done up to present, which by all accounts were very few, had been beset with problems like language difficulties, misunderstandings, and in some cases, abuse over payments.

As we chatted on, he suggested that if I was interested in going into the grant business he could introduce me as his friend to some of the community, but in return I would have to do his grant job solely for the grant money, which at that time would save him in the region of £3,000.

The major problem for a lot of the builders was the householder's final payment on completion of the works, which would normally come as a low cost mortgage from the council, and nine times out of ten It would have been signed over to the builder on starting the works.

Now, you would think that after signing these contracts, they would be binding on the owner to pay, providing, of course, he received his final certificate which the council's own inspectors had to supply him with, "stating that all works that had been carried out by the builder had been passed by the council" Bearing this in mind you wouldn't think there would be any problem between builder and owner at the end of the day.

Ha ha ha! Apparently what some of our Asian friends were doing was waiting until the majority of the work had been done, for which the builder would have received part-payment from the grant allowance, and then without the builder's knowledge, the Asians would then return to the council and rescind their mortgage agreement and there was nothing the council could do about it.

The builder would normally not find out about the problem for a couple of weeks, which would give the Asian plenty of time to bugger off back to Pakistan where the hard-working builder would be unable to take him to court, or even the opportunity to kick the bastard's brains in, which he rightly deserved.

The only comment I can make concerning the council at the time is that, they were the biggest load of wankers I have ever had the misfortune to come across in my life. The biggest wanker of all was the boss of the Environmental Health department, a little prat by the name of Littlemore. That aside, I made a deal with my Asian friend that I would do his work for the grant money, but before that could come about he had to find me four other

Asian clients, tied up legally, and on top of that if I had any problems with any of them he would be on hand to sort them out, which fair play to him, as time went by, he did so on numerous occasions.

If you can just think about the predicament that I had chosen to put myself in – all of a sudden I had five contracts to start, more or less together, and didn't know a fucking thing about the building trade, not even to the point of mixing a bit of compo!

The work I had signed up for was worth in the region of £50,000, and for that I had to supply five houses with a new damp course, kitchen extension, replastering, outside rendering, rewiring, etc. What a bloody nightmare I had created for myself! Later on, when I was discussing the events that led up to me stepping into the building trade with a friend over a beer, my mate summed up what had happened in these few words, 'Charlie, if you are a full shilling, I know where there's a fucking house full!' I think perhaps he wasn't far wrong.

Apart from the many problems I had at the time, the main one was not having the capital to finance the works, so it was off to the bank manager for a business loan, which I am glad to say there was no problem with, but only for the fact that I had recently put £12,000 cash down on my new home which left the bank with more than ample security. With the money now sorted out, I managed to find some subcontractors to sort out the different aspects of the works, leaving me with the question, should I do the building work, one property at a time, or stick my neck out, balls included, and start work on all five. I think, on reflection, it was one of the few times in my life that I must have realized what a Kamikaze pilot felt like as he went into his death dive.

While trying to make my mind up, over the amount of properties to start on, my mates – who, I have no doubt, meant well at the time - were telling me to leave it alone, and stick to my decorating or I would go bump, and lose the lot, which didn't help considering the pressure that was on me at the time.

Fuck them all! I started the five together, working day and night, and to say thc first couplc of months were a nightmare would be the understatement of the century.

By the time I was two thirds of the way through my first five houses, I had started another three or four. By the time I had finished my first five, I was doing ten at a time, and so it went on to the point that I had thirty on the go. The money, by this time, was flying in and out, and while it was in I started to buy derelict properties in the grant areas, and more than managed to complete them for the grant money.

The only problem with builders having grants on their properties was the fact that they would then have to keep them for a minimum of five years, or repay the grant.

Another stipulation where builders were concerned was that they had to make their houses that had grants on them available to the public on six monthly rentals at the going rates of the new Fair Rents Board, which once it had come into force, wasn't bad.

If for some reason you sold the property before the five years were up, you had to repay the full grant money you had received, plus interest, so it was a no- go where selling them was concerned.

Over the couple of years I was doing the grant works I made many new acquaintances, some good, and some not so! With most of them being in businesses that were based in Manchester, and every now and then I would receive a telephone call telling me that they would be having a get together on such and such a day. These get-togethers were totally private, and I emphasize the word private, and always held somewhere in Manchester. They would normally cost you in the region of £60 or more, and in that price, apart from your food and drink, the leg-over, if required; with what were always smart sexy young ladies. One of the main things that went on there, apart from the sex and drink, was the business that was carried out under the table.

These private meetings were always held during the week, and usually lasted most of the day. The reason they were always held on a weekday, was so it wouldn't interfere with anybody's family life at the weekends. It was at one of these meetings that I met, and became friends with, a well-educated chap, who I believed to be a Jew, and a very rich one at that.

I later bought a second-hand Gold Coloured Silver Shadow Rolls Royce at a knock down price with my personalised number plate, from him. Although at the time I wasn't really interested in football I acquired two private seats at Manchester United, mainly to be used for people I wanted to butter up, and could possibly do me a favour where my business was concerned, always, of course, taking them in the Rolls.

At United, if you have personalized seats, there was also a high-class private restaurant where a meal before the match would cost you up to £40 a head. I would often, apart from meeting my friends there for lunch, take people like the bank manager, building inspectors, councillors or anyone else who could be of service to me at the time.

I had been in the building trade for less than five years, and had accumulated in the region of 15 apartments, five stone houses and a 28-bedroom hostel' and believe it or not, it wasn't until one sunny Friday afternoon when I was sitting on my front lawn, feeling once again completely knackered, that my wife came out with a bottle of bubbly, and two glasses. When I asked her what we were celebrating, she handed me a glass and said to me, 'Here's to us, love! We have made it!'

Now, my friends, to get to where I did, I believe I couldn't have done it, without the help of the fucking devil, that I had somehow known from day one was perched on my shoulder.

Two Years Later I was Divorced Bankrupt and Penniless!

That bastard was still on my shoulder.......

Beware my friends of the Devil!
For you may be next!